PLANTBASED
ALEXANDER GERSHBERG

~~~

To Ben,
For your warmth,
for your love,
for many moments of joy you brought into my life,
for the wonderful man you grew up to be

PLANTBASED

80 NOURISHING,
UMAMI-RICH RECIPES
FROM THE KITCHEN OF
A PASSIONATE CHEF

Alexander
Gershberg

Smith
Street
Books

Contents

~~~

My little plant-based kitchen   P 7

    Whole grains   P 25

    Beans & proteins   P 73

    Root vegetables   P 121

    Sweet round vegetables   P 147

    Green vegetables   P 189

    Sea vegetables   P 213

    Pickles & fermentation   P 231

    Fruits & desserts   P 251

Sample menus   P 285

Special ingredients   P 287

Shops & online stores   P 291

Sources & further reading   P 295

Thanks   P 297

My little plant-based kitchen   P 301

Index   P 302

MY LITTLE
PLANT-BASED KITCHEN

My little plant-based kitchen

ALEXANDER
GERSHBERG

~~~

I've lived in this city for 15 years, always in small apartments with small, quirky kitchens. When friends came over, my kitchen would be exploding with hundreds of colours of ingredients and often it would be impossible to see the counter. Everyone would wonder how I managed to cook all these dishes in that tiny kitchen. I managed, just like I managed to cater for 100 people from the very same little plant-based kitchen.

As happens often in cities like this to broke poor artists like myself, I've been thrown out of where I used to live too many times. So what did I do? I took a vigorous and deep breath, puffed my chest out, stuck my nose up towards the grey Amsterdam sky, rented a *bakfiets* (Dutch cargo bike) and moved to a new place in a new neighbourhood. How exciting, I thought — barely managing to stop my chest from collapsing — I will explore another neighbourhood of this city. I will again explore a tiny kitchen. I will make it my own. I will dwell in it with all my ingredients, my herbs, my dry grains and my ferments. In no time, I would turn it into own tiny, messy, colourful, wonderful, cosmopolitan little plant-based kitchen.

I remember one kitchen when I lived on the Tuinstraat in the Jordaan, in *het liefdehofje* (the love yard). After 10 minutes of cooking, I would realise I was out of space. There I made my first plant-based meals, there I always came back from dance rehearsals exhausted. There was love, there were friends, there was a budding dance career, there were dishes that were popping out of a huge mess, there I dreamt for the first time of becoming a professional chef.

The most exciting thing happening in that kitchen was the baking. The toy toaster oven that my mother bought for me dominated with its heavy weight on top of a fragile and small wooden bookcase I had found in the street. There were two things to pay attention to: you needed a knife and a prayer for this kid-sized oven to agree to open and, while opening it, the whole wooden bookshelf construction would start to tilt towards you and almost collapse. With your well-practised and skillful baker's hand, you had to stop the heavy bookshelf from falling and the oven batting into the faces of your guests. This operation often worked. My first attempts at vegan baking, though, often didn't.

There were no schools for plant-based cooking at that time but I — naive and optimistic — wanted to become a chef. I had to figure it out all by myself. With a bunch of dull and grey macrobiotic books, no income, an oven that was a daily hazard and plenty of hungry friends, I was a silly, unrealistic dancer kid who wanted to become a chef. Looking back, I sometimes wonder, 'What was I thinking?'

Apart from my own little kitchen, I saw many kitchens when I was cooking for my private clients. Some were as tiny as mine and some were the best-equipped fancy kitchens at yet another fairytale castle in the Dutch countryside. After this kitchen, came another plant-based kitchen, and another one and another one. Wherever I was, I never needed or used fancy equipment. I never needed anything special. I always made do with what was there. No matter how big or small the client's kitchen was, they were always apologising to me that their kitchen was too small for me. 'You have no idea what kitchen I am cooking in every day,' I thought. 'I'll do my best,' I answered and smiled politely.

If you want to, and you dream big, many things are possible. From my little plant-based kitchen, I cooked thousands of meals for thousands of people. From my little plant-based kitchen, one meal at a time, I decided to change the world. From my little plant-based, inner-city kitchen, I decided to make the world a better place to be.

WHY I CHOSE TO BECOME
A PLANT-BASED CHEF

I was a young, rather naive and outrageously ambitious dancer.
When my friends went out to clubs, trying and experiencing everything
people that age do, I cooked miso soups, fermented vegetables,
pressure-cooked brown rice and Hokkaido soy beans, and made
seaweed dishes inspired by shojin ryiori, the traditional Japanese temple
cuisine. I was a weirdo. At 26, as a young chef, I was cooking without sugar,
dairy products, eggs or the holy grail of the Dutch eating culture —
cheese. I was claiming shamelessly that this would be the future of food.

In 2008, fermentation was considered a funky occupation, whole grains
such as millet were just food for birds and desserts without sugar were
usually reserved for a few unenthusiastic health fanatics. To do what
I did — to take a stand against the raised eyebrows of my family, the
artists lifestyle of my friends and colleagues, and the rejection of other
chefs — took courage, determination and conviction in what I stood for.
What I still stand for. My radical choices were a result of few realisations
that I still believe and that I will share with you in this book.

I only learned how powerful food can be after I suffered from a chronic
skin disease for many months, without being able to find a cure for it.
I was amazed that it took only one week of eating a healthy, wholefoods,
plant-based diet, for my skin condition to vanish. My initial inspiration
and the knowledge I gained came from macrobiotics (an Eastern
philosophy and way of eating based on the principles of yin and
yang), through which I learned how crucial what we eat can be for
our health and for preventing and reversing chronic illnesses. Years
later, scientific research and articles have been published about
food and its underestimated role in our health and mental wellbeing.

As I write these lines, it has been 15 years since I started eating in a
macrobiotic way. For 15 years, I have noticed how my health, strength,
vitality and flexibility have improved. I'm more energised and a happier
person than I was 15 years ago. I'm stronger and more flexible in my
yoga and dance practices than I was when I was a young professional
dancer and, as I rarely get sick, I haven't seen my doctor for a long time.
The realisation of how much of a role diet plays in our health and what
great potential it has in solving the high rates of sickness that seem to
be present in our lives nowadays, motivated me to pursue a career
as a chef and a cooking teacher.

Simply speaking, highly processed foods and animal foods in the modern diet, when eaten for a long time, can cause chronic diseases, such as diabetes, cancer, heart disease, high blood pressure, high cholesterol and obesity — the main causes of premature deaths. Plant-based, wholefoods diets have been linked to significantly lower incidences of chronic sickness, while animal-based foods are often linked to higher incidences (see 'Sources & further reading' on page 295). As most of the world's population is struggling with these diseases, and almost no family remains untouched, the solution is very simple and just under our noses: the food we are eating makes us sick. The medical and scientific world has failed to combat these chronic sicknesses and the rate of people getting ill is getting higher with every decade. Changing our food habits into one based on whole, plant-based foods can dramatically assist in the prevention of the majority of these sicknesses, and even the reversal of some.

As I started to eat more wholefood, plant-based foods and my diet became cleaner, I noticed that my mind became clearer, my thinking became sharper and, in general, I experienced fewer symptoms of ailments I'd had in the past. This is a very satisfying and gratifying journey and I hear the same story often from people who are following this lifestyle and diet.

Many people choose to eat a plant-based diet because of the negative impact that an animal-based diet has on the environment and the devastating effect it has on the life (and death) of the animals abused in this cruel industry. I definitely support these two causes strongly and I'm certain you can find a lot of information about them, but not in this book. In this cookbook, I focus on the culinary, nutritional, health and wellbeing aspects of a plant-based diet, and the joy and pleasure of cooking. These are my fields of expertise and what I'm most passionate about.

My unique standpoint towards nutrition is that I combine it with my knowledge about the energetical properties of food that I've studied through macrobiotics and traditional Chinese medicine. By combining these two fields — traditional and modern, Eastern and Western — I present a full scope and overview of how you can use foods for your own daily benefit.

If you asked me why I chose to become a plant-based chef, I would say that I did it to inspire people to eat a healthy diet that will make them feel good, look good, be energised and contribute to the prevention of chronic sicknesses (or reverse them). This solution is simple, but it requires knowledge and skill to cook delicious, satisfying and attractive plant-based meals. When you know how to cook plant-based meals in an attractive and delicious way, you're more likely to make a quicker transition into plant-based eating. By cooking these impressive meals for your family and friends, you will also attract more people around you towards a healthier way of eating. Cooking is your secret weapon. Cooking delicious food can change the world one meal at a time!

HOW TO COOK AMAZING MEALS
FROM A TINY PLANT-BASED KITCHEN

Most people think that you need a grand kitchen and fancy equipment to cook a good meal. In fact, all you really need is a source of fire, a cutting board, a knife and pan (and preferably a pressure cooker). I assure you that you can prepare most of the recipes in this book with the help of these tools only. These are mainly what I use to prepare my daily meals. I strongly believe that what makes your meal really good is not fancy equipment, but a few basic principles that I learned from cooking professionally. I am going to share them with you. These are my secrets for good cooking:

1 ～～～
The best produce and ingredients

I always cook with organic ingredients. This is how all the recipes in this cookbook were created. On the rare occasions that I cooked something with ingredients bought at a supermarket, my food just didn't taste as good, no matter how much effort, love and attention I put into it. This is how I realised how much my cooking and its success is really dependent on the quality of the produce. Most food from mass-produced agriculture is grown with pesticides, chemicals and artificial fertilisers. When grown in poor-quality soil, these foods lack flavour and are different in quality in comparison to foods that were grown on organic soil full of minerals and bacteria. For this reason, I encourage you to buy organic and good–quality produce.

If you are not used to shopping for organic produce, you can start by ordering a weekly box of organic fruits and vegetables from a local farmer. Usually these boxes are quite affordable. Otherwise, you can shop at a farmers' market, or even better, grow (some of) your own vegetables yourself. Or simply shop at an organic store.

The reward for cooking with organic ingredients (both fresh and dry) is enormous. The food will taste much better and will do much more for your body.

2 ~~~
Fire

Fire was first used by humans for cooking about 1.8 million years ago. After this, we started to digest food quicker, which allowed more time and energy for socialising and thinking. This was also the period when our brain grew larger. Fire is an essential element in our human development.

When I worked as a private chef, I noticed that many households have shifted to induction stoves in the last few years. Personally, when I cook on an electric or induction stove, I can really feel how it impacts the taste and the culinary experience of the dish. I can feel how the taste will not be as strong and the energy of the dish will be weak and low. In the few occasions that I did cook on an electric or induction stove I tended to feel physically weaker, lacking energy and vitality. What I was actually missing is fire!

Cooking with fire gives strength, energy, warmth. It mobilises processes in all the body's systems. The blood system, the lymphatic system, the nervous system and the digestive system. Fire creates movements and dynamics and it stimulates passion and hunger for life. Cooking with fire brings a spark to the eyes.

For many people, the change to a fire stove is difficult. To help my clients adjust, we buy a 4-burner camping gas stove (with a gas bottle attached) that we place just on top of their induction plate. I cook meals for them on it and I encourage them to cook on it too. It is incredible to see how much better they felt, even after one meal.

3 〜〜

Love, attention, intention, energy, feeling

When I'm cooking, I am checking with myself: is my body calm, is my posture elongated, is my breath calm, am I enjoying it? Am I sending my love to the people that I am cooking for?

Good cooking — real cooking — comes from the heart. Cooking is an intimate act done for the people you love as an act of nourishment and support. The way you stand in the kitchen, the way you breathe, the way you look, smell, touch and taste should all be done from the most loving, pure, calm intention. Cooking should not involve stress or anger, or any desire to get something out of it. This is a principle I teach my students. I teach them to move in the kitchen with calmness and love, to feel the food, to bring attention, love and generosity into every movement, to every vegetable they cut and every stir-fry they mix. The love and good energy that you put into a dish will transform it and can potentially make all the difference between good cooking and bad cooking.

4 〜〜

Knowledge, skill and technique

To make a sustainable transition into a plant-based lifestyle, it is essential that you learn how to create daily menus and how to cook plant-based foods. Many people make the transition to a plant-based diet but lack the basic knowledge and skill to maintain it in a sustainable way for their health in the longer term. You need to know about the nutritional values of foods and which ingredients you should cook with to get these nutrients. But you also need to know how to cook them to optimise their digestion, nourishment and taste. If you don't have this basic knowledge, your meals may not only be nutritionally deficient but also unfulfilling on a culinary level. Giving you the essential knowledge for eating a plant-based diet is one of the main reasons I have written this book.

5 〰〰
A pressure cooker and a good knife

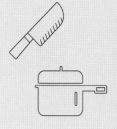

These are investments I recommend to everyone. Pressure cooking makes whole grains and beans more digestible and softer, which makes the nutrients more available to our body. It also makes the digestion process easier. Since a pressure cooker reduces the cooking time of grains and beans and makes eating them more pleasant, it also makes it more likely that you will incorporate the habits of cooking grains and beans into your daily life.

I cut all the vegetables and fruits in this book by hand. Buying a good knife is essential for enjoying cutting, gaining good cutting skills and cutting the vegetables properly. The quality of cut vegetables really makes a difference in how the dish tastes and feels. If the vegetables are cut in a chaotic, uneven way, it impacts the taste and the whole experience of the dish. When you are very clear about your cutting, the dish will look and taste better and you will feel better. I recommend a thin Japanese vegetable knife, for example, a nakiri knife or santoku knife.

In general, my recipes do not require complicated equipment or fancy machines, but I highly recommend you invest in these two tools to optimise your use of this cookbook.

A NOTE ON THE PREPARATION
AND WAIT TIMES IN RECIPES

〰〰

In this book, the preparation time includes the time it takes to prepare each ingredient, as well as any cooking that takes place alongside. For example, if you're preparing a salad while another part of the dish is already cooking on the stovetop, the cook time will form a part of this preparation time and won't be listed separately.

The wait time refers to how long you have to wait for something to cook and your hands are free. ▪

THE PLANT-BASED PLATE

I can't overemphasise how important it is to eat a daily diet that is whole and complete on a nutritional basis. It will give you the energy, strength and nutrition so you feel good and can be vital, which will encourage you to keep going with a plant-based lifestyle. A deficient plant-based diet, based on meat and dairy replacements and manufactured supermarket products, is not nourishing enough for your body. People who eat like this are very likely to stop plant-based eating sooner or later.

The chart overleaf shows you the ultimate balanced plant-based food pattern. It also gives a good example of what your plate could look like. Every chapter in this book is based on one of the main components in this chart. I will explain them in more detail in the introduction to each chapter.

This chart is based on the nutritional knowledge that I have gained over many years, the macrobiotic diet, the Mediterranean diet and Harvard University's medical school ideal food diagram (see 'Sources & further reading' on page 295).

Whole grains and legumes

Together, whole grains and legumes form 'complete proteins'. In other words, they provide all the essential amino acids that the body needs for regular functioning. Whole grains, or products made from whole grains, should be eaten in every meal. Legumes should be eaten at least once a day. Complementary sources of protein include tofu, tempeh, seitan and natto, which you can combine in your meals on a daily basis.

Vegetables

Vegetables provide the body with minerals and vitamins. There are three kinds of vegetables that should be eaten in every meal:

1. vegetables that grow beneath the ground — root vegetables
2. vegetables that grow at ground level — sweet, round vegetables
3. vegetables that grow above the ground — green vegetables

Whole grains, legumes and vegetables form the main pillars of the plant-based cuisine and should be eaten every day. They also contain complex carbohydrates, which give a slow and steady supply of energy to your body.

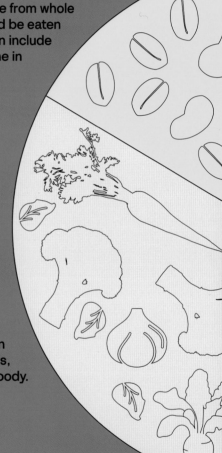

Next to whole grains, legumes and vegetables, there a few
components that are essential for daily use, but don't form
the main portion on the plate. They should be eaten every
day, but are not the main course. These are:

— seaweeds, which are rich in iron
and calcium and other minerals
— fermented foods, which help digestion and
the absorption of nutrients into the body
— seeds and nuts, which are rich in necessary
oils and certain beneficial minerals
— fruits and dried fruits, which also
contain a lot of vitamins and minerals

~~~
Important note

There are a few nutrients that are missing in
a plant-based diet or are more challenging for
the body to assimilate. I am mainly talking here
about vitamin B12, although some nutritionists
also mention vitamin D and omega 3 in this regard.
Vitamin D can be easily obtained by regular exposure
to direct sunlight and omega 3 is present in green
vegetables, beans and seeds. To compensate for this,
some people, like myself, choose to eat small amounts
of animal protein, like fish, alongside a plant-based diet.
This works well for me. Others choose to take supplements,
which I am personally not fond of because they are highly
processed and can cause many unbalances in the body. Each
of these choices comes with disadvantages. I can't tell you how to
solve this problem and I am not sure that I have found the right answer
to it myself. I do hope you find a way that works for you. ∎

# WHOLE

# GRAINS

# Whole grains

~~~~

Whole grains are the edible seeds of specific cereal grasses belonging to the *Poaceae* (formerly known as *Gramineae*) family. Research has shown that, throughout history, humans who lived in nomadic societies were more gatherers than hunters. Apart from seeds, nuts and fruits, people were also gathering wild whole grains. Following the agricultural revolution 12,000 years ago, whole grains became domesticated. We learned how to grow them on a large scale so they can supply us with the nutrients we need.

In ancient cultures like Mesopotamia, whole grains were such a staple that people used them as a currency to trade goods with. The most sophisticated, intellectual and technologically advanced cultures of recorded history developed around the culture of cultivating and being nourished by whole grains. Look, for example, at Ancient Mesopotamia, Ancient Greece, Ancient Egypt and Ancient China, where philosophy, medicines, mathematics, astrology, astronomy, physics and sciences developed. It was millet and rice in China, buckwheat in Russia, barley and rye in Europe, wheat in the Middle East, sorghum in Africa and corn in South and Central America. In all these cultures, whole grains were the main staple foods.

Whole grains are a very rich source of nutrition. They contain essential amino acids (proteins), complex carbohydrates, minerals, fibre and B group vitamins. When you start to realise the enormous nutritional benefits and the great potential of whole grains, it is incomprehensible that they are so scarce in the modern diet. Whole grains are so nutritionally dense and powerful that they can nourish whole communities, societies and civilisations.

Besides their nutritional properties, whole grains are very strengthening and provide a steady supply of stable energy to the body. Whole grains strengthen the core of the body — the intestinal area, the hara chakra. They give us the strength and the ability to work hard, to stand firm on both feet, to concentrate and to have a clear goal in life. Whole grains are also good for clear intellectual thinking and philosophising. No wonder the most sophisticated philosophies and complex technologies have developed in societies where whole grains were the staple food.

Nowadays, few people are eating whole grains, are aware of their benefits or know how to use and cook them. One of the goals of this book is to encourage you to fall in love with whole grains, to get familiar with them and to implement whole grains in your daily cooking routine. I describe how to cook whole grains in the recipes in this chapter.

I highly encourage you to use a pressure cooker for cooking whole grains. The pressure cooker breaks the structure of the grain and makes it softer, easier to digest and more pleasant to eat, while still keeping its whole structure. Pressure cooking will also allow the body to better absorb the nutrients from the cooked grains. On page 69, I describe how to cook brown rice, and you can also apply this to other grains.

Whole grains, beans and vegetables, are rich in complex carbohydrates. Unfortunately — and unfairly — many people avoid eating carbohydrates. Most people don't distinguish between simple and complex carbohydrates. Simple carbohydrates (from sugar, honey, sweets and processed white flour foods) digest quickly and are stored in the body as fat. Complex carbohydrates digest slowly and supply a slow, steady stream of glucose into the blood. This constant supply of sugars to the bloodstream results in a stable balanced energy and mood. Complex carbohydrates won't make you fat, but they will give you energy to move and live life with more vitality.

Whole grains should be at the centre of each meal. They will provide balance, a solid base and strength to each meal. In a wholefoods, plant-based diet, no meal is complete without a whole grain. A sustainable and sensible transition to a plant-based diet will not be done by implementing highly-processed meat and dairy replacements, which are harmful to our health. A transition to a plant-based diet can be done by familiarising yourself with foods such as whole grains. They are easy to grow, nutritionally dense and affordable. Whole grains can feed the whole world's population and provide it with the proper nutrition that it needs.

I worry when I see the highly-processed meat and milk replacement (although there is nothing wrong with homemade ones) market gaining in popularity and being presented as the way to transition to a plant-based diet. This is not the solution — these products are harmful to our bodies. Whole grains, on the other hand, are the exact opposite. There is no company, no cooperative and no marketing campaign that will tell you that. But I will continue to persuade you, remind you and hopefully help you realise that whole grains are the food of the future. ▪

Farro salad with pumpkin, colourful beetroot & cherry tomatoes

Serves 4
Preparation time: 45 minutes

INGREDIENTS

- 250 g (9 oz) farro grande (pearled spelt)
- sea salt
- 1 small Hokkaido pumpkin or any other variety (about 750 g/1 lb 11 oz), unpeeled, cut into large chunks
- 75 ml (2½ fl oz) olive oil
- black pepper
- ¾ teaspoon pul biber (Aleppo pepper)
- 2½ tablespoons pure maple syrup
- 50 g (⅓ cup) almonds, roughly chopped
- 1 yellow beetroot (beet), peeled and thinly sliced
- 1 pink target (Chioggia) beetroot (beet), peeled and thinly sliced
- 300 g (10½ oz) cherry tomatoes, halved
- 20 g (⅓ cup) roughly chopped dill fronds
- 2 tablespoons umesu
- 1 tablespoon freshly squeezed lemon juice

It was the end of September. The warm days were getting a bit colder but the memories of the lazy summer kept on clinging to us. There were still great tomatoes available on the market and the first beetroot and pumpkins were delicious, fresh and juicy. I would go to the market once a week and come back with enormous bags bursting with juicy and colourful vegetables.

It was Rosh HaShana, Jewish New Year, and I was very late to my friends' house to make dinner. When I started to cook, I knew everyone was already waiting at the dinner table. 'Cook quick, go quick', I thought and, without noticing, I started to improvise with all the colourful vegetables that were resting in the kitchen and asking for attention. I worked quickly and didn't think. I just put all the tasty stuff together in one dish.

By the time we were eating around the festive table, everyone forgave me for coming so late, but only after they took the first bite. 'Something for the next cookbook?', a friend asked while chewing, and the atmosphere seemed warmer and easier.

Spelt is an ancient variety of wheat that is more digestible than normal wheat. It has sweet and sour notes — I find it extremely tasty and the texture is really appealing and interesting. When I eat it, I wonder why everyone is not using it regularly. You can find it in most organic food stores.

Farro grande is the Italian name for spelt or pearled spelt. In this recipe I use pearled spelt because it is lighter, sweeter and the bite is nicer than whole spelt. You can also replace pearled spelt in this salad with pearled barley. Whole spelt remains very hard even after long cooking, so I usually don't use it.

METHOD

Place the farro in a pressure cooker, cover with plenty of water and use your hands to swirl the grains in a gentle, circular motion. Drain the farro and repeat the process until the water runs clear.

Return the farro to the pressure cooker, add 375 ml (1½ cups) of water and a pinch of salt, then cover and secure the pressure cooker lid. Place the pressure cooker over high heat and allow to come to medium pressure. Reduce the heat to low and place the cooker on top of a flame deflector (this will prevent the pressure increasing too much). Cook for 45 minutes, then turn off the heat and allow the pressure to release naturally. Transfer the farro to a salad bowl.

Meanwhile, preheat the oven to 180°C (350°F) fan-forced.

Place the pumpkin on a baking tray, drizzle over 60 ml (¼ cup) of the olive oil and season generously with salt and pepper. Transfer to the oven and roast for 30–45 minutes, or until golden brown. Remove the tray from the oven, sprinkle over ½ teaspoon of the pul biber and drizzle with 1½ tablespoons of the maple syrup, then roast for a further 2 minutes.

Heat the remaining 1 tablespoon of oil in a small saucepan over medium heat. Add the almonds and cook for about 2 minutes, until golden, taking care not to burn them and reducing the heat if necessary. Add the remaining ¼ teaspoon of pul biber and remaining 1 tablespoon of maple syrup and cook for another minute until most of the liquid has evaporated. Immediately remove the almonds from the pan and wash the pan while the caramel is still warm so it doesn't stick once cooled.

Fill a saucepan with 1 cm (½ in) of water, add a pinch of salt and bring to the boil. Add the yellow beetroot and cook over medium heat for 5–6 minutes, until just tender but still al dente. Using a slotted spoon, transfer the yellow beetroot to the salad bowl with the farro and repeat with the pink beetroot.

Add the pumpkin, almonds, cherry tomato, dill, umesu and lemon juice to the salad bowl and gently toss to combine. Serve with pleasure and love. ∎

Brown rice pilaf with broccoli & shiitake mushrooms

~~~~~~~~~~

Serves 4
Preparation time: 30 minutes
Wait time: 45 minutes

INGREDIENTS

- 8 dried shiitake mushrooms
- 225 g (1 cup) brown short-grain rice
- 75 g (2¾ oz) brown sweet rice
- 50 g (⅓ cup) pine nuts
- sea salt
- 1 head of broccoli (about 500 g/ 1 lb 2 oz), cut into small florets
- 1 tablespoon roasted sesame oil
- 90 ml (3 fl oz) mirin
- 1 tablespoon brown rice vinegar
- 1 tablespoon shoyu

This dish is simple, daily, elegant and nourishing. The textures create a very calm and pleasant mouth feel. Brown rice is a very strengthening grain, especially good for the intestines and the lower abdomen. Brown rice gives clarity of thinking, discipline and focus. You can eat this dish when you want to feel balanced and centred.

METHOD

Soak the shiitake mushrooms in 200 ml (7 fl oz) of water for 30 minutes. Pressure cook the rice in 475 ml (16 fl oz) of water, following the instructions on page 69.

Meanwhile, place the pine nuts in a frying pan over medium heat and toast, stirring constantly, for 3–5 minutes, until golden brown, taking care not to burn them and reducing the heat if necessary. Immediately transfer the pine nuts to a small bowl.

Bring 1.5 litres (6 cups) of water to the boil over high heat. Add a pinch of salt and the broccoli and cook for 1–2 minutes, until bright green but still retaining some crunch. Watch carefully because this will happen very quickly. Drain the broccoli, then return it to the pan and set over high heat. Add the sesame oil, 3 tablespoons of the mirin and ¼ teaspoon of salt, and sauté for 1 minute.

If the shiitake mushrooms have softened, remove the hard stems and slice the mushroom caps. If they are still hard, transfer to a small saucepan, along with the soaking liquid, and bring to a simmer over low heat. Cook for 5–10 minutes or until the mushrooms are soft, then remove from the pan, remove the stems and thinly slice the caps. Return the mushrooms to the pan with the soaking liquid, add the remaining 3 tablespoons of mirin, the brown rice vinegar and shoyu and cook for 5–10 minutes, until most of the liquid has evaporated.

Combine the rice, broccoli, mushrooms and pine nuts in a serving bowl and serve warm or at room temperature. ∎

Brown rice pilaf with cherry tomatoes & chanterelles

~~~~~~~~~~

Serves 4
Preparation time: 15 minutes
Wait time: 45 minutes

INGREDIENTS

- 180 g (6½ oz) brown short-grain rice
- 90 g (3 oz) brown sweet rice
- 3 tablespoons olive oil
- 1 leek, trimmed, white and green parts thinly sliced into rounds
- 350 g (12½ oz) chanterelle mushrooms
- 500 g (1 lb 2 oz) cherry tomatoes, halved
- 1 garlic clove, finely grated
- ¼ teaspoon chilli flakes
- ¼ teaspoon sea salt
- black pepper, to taste

My friend Ingrid came by in the middle of the night and I wanted to prepare something nice but really quick for her. I had rice, chanterelle mushrooms and cherry tomatoes.

'This dish has all my favourite ingredients,' Ingrid said. 'How did you know?'

'I just felt it, felt you.'

This kind of dish reminds me that fresh, healthy cooking at home can be easy, quick and done without too much fuss. You can do it in no time when you are cooking for someone you love.

Many people throw away the green part of the leek but, besides being edible, it is tasty and nutritious. Please make sure you use it in this recipe. I use chanterelle mushrooms, but you can easily replace these with any other type of mushrooms. Oyster mushrooms will work just as well. Although it takes 45 minutes to pressure cook the rice, finishing the dish is really quick. It only takes 5–10 minutes to produce a very tasty stir-fry. You can also use left-over brown rice. Go for it!

METHOD

Pressure cook the rice in 400 ml (14 fl oz) of water, following the instructions on page 69.

Heat the olive oil in a large frying pan over medium–high heat. When the oil is hot, add the leek and sauté for 1 minute or until starting to soften, then add the mushrooms, tomato, garlic, chilli flakes, sea salt and a generous amount of black pepper. Sauté, stirring, for 3 minutes. Add the cooked rice and sauté for a further 2–3 minutes, then divide among plates and serve with love. ■

Creamy polenta with roasted mushrooms & spinach

~~~

Serves 4
Preparation time: 20 minutes
Wait time: 30 minutes–2 hours

INGREDIENTS

- sea salt
- 90 ml (3 fl oz) olive oil
- 150 g (1 cup) polenta
- 1 onion, thinly sliced into half moons
- 500 g (1 lb 2 oz) mixed mushrooms, such as button, shiitake, portobello, oyster mushrooms, thickly sliced
- 5 g (¼ oz) sage leaves
- 2 garlic cloves, finely chopped
- black pepper
- 150 g (3 cups firmly packed) spinach, washed

This dish is real comfort food. The creamy polenta is complemented by the mushrooms and spinach, which add another layer of smoothness to indulge in. Don't be afraid to cook the polenta for a very long time, even up to a few hours. It gets better with time.

METHOD

Combine 750 ml (3 cups) of water, ½ teaspoon of salt and 3 tablespoons of the olive oil in a saucepan and bring to the boil. Slowly pour in the polenta in a steady stream, whisking constantly to avoid the polenta forming lumps and sticking to the base of the pan. Once you've added all the polenta, continue to whisk until the mixture comes to a gentle boil. Cover the pan, reduce the heat to medium–low and simmer for at least 30 minutes, stirring the polenta every 5–10 minutes. If you have the time and patience, you can cook the polenta for up to a few hours; the longer you cook it, the tastier, sweeter, creamier and more comforting it will be — I like to cook it for about 2 hours. The polenta should stay smooth and creamy throughout cooking, but if it becomes too thick, add a little water every once in a while.

Heat 2 tablespoons of the remaining olive oil in a frying pan over high heat. Add the onion and sauté for 1–2 minutes, until slightly golden, then add the mushrooms, sage, garlic, ½ teaspoon of salt and a generous grind of black pepper, and sauté for 5 minutes. Add the remaining 1 tablespoon of olive oil if the pan starts to look dry. Add the spinach and another ¼ teaspoon of salt and continue to sauté for 2 minutes or until the spinach has wilted.

Ladle the polenta onto plates, top with the vegetable mixture and serve. ▪

Couscous pilaf with roasted cauliflower & pine nuts

~~~~~~~~~~

Serves 4
Preparation time: 20 minutes
Wait time: 30 minutes

INGREDIENTS

- 1 head of cauliflower, cut into florets
- 60 ml (¼ cup) olive oil
- ½ teaspoon coarse sea salt
- black pepper

VEGETABLE COUSCOUS

- 250 g (1⅓ cups) couscous
- sea salt and black pepper
- 3 tablespoons olive oil
- 30 g (1 oz) pine nuts
- 1 zucchini (courgette), sliced in half lengthways, then cut into 1 cm (½ in) thick half moons
- bunch of parsley (about 70 g/2½ oz), chopped
- 150 g (5½ oz) sweetcorn kernels
- 100 g (3½ oz) black olives, roughly chopped
- 1 tablespoon freshly squeezed lemon juice
- ground sumac, to serve

This is an extremely simple and very tasty dish that you can easily make for a quick lunch or dinner. With so many tasty elements in one dish, you can't really go wrong.

METHOD

Preheat the oven to 180°C (350°F) fan-forced.

Place the cauliflower on a baking tray and drizzle the olive oil over the top. Sprinkle with the coarse sea salt and season with a generous amount of black pepper. Transfer to the oven and roast for 30–45 minutes, until dark brown.

To make the couscous, bring 350 ml (12 fl oz) of water to the boil in a small saucepan. Place the couscous, ¼ teaspoon of sea salt, a generous amount of black pepper and 1 tablespoon of the olive oil in a salad bowl. Use a fork to evenly distribute the oil through the couscous, then pour over the boiling water — it should be just a little higher than the height of the couscous. Cover the bowl with a plate or lid, then set aside to steam for about 10 minutes. Remove the lid and lightly fluff the grains with the fork.

Heat a small saucepan over medium heat, add the pine nuts and toast, stirring constantly to avoid them burning and adjusting the heat if necessary, for 2 minutes or until golden. Immediately transfer the pine nuts to a small bowl.

Heat a frying pan over high heat and add the remaining 2 tablespoons of olive oil. Add the zucchini and parsley and sauté for 1–2 minutes, then season with ¼ teaspoon of sea salt and a generous grind of black pepper. The zucchini should be shiny and still crisp.

Add the roasted cauliflower, pine nuts, zucchini and parsley, sweetcorn, black olives, lemon juice and a sprinkle of sumac to the couscous. Toss to combine, then dig in and have fun. ∎

Barley pilaf with cherry tomatoes & seitan

~~~~~~~~

Serves 4
Preparation time: 10 minutes
Wait time: 45 minutes

INGREDIENTS

- 250 g (9 oz) pearl barley
- 500–750 ml (2–3 cups) organic sunflower oil, for deep-frying
- 350 g (12½ oz) seitan, cut in chunks
- 2 tablespoons olive oil
- 2 onions, thinly sliced into half moons
- sea salt
- 500 g (1 lb 2 oz) cherry tomatoes, halved
- 75 g (2¾ oz) rocket (arugula) or turnip greens, roughly chopped
- 2 garlic cloves, grated
- black pepper
- 1 tablespoon freshly squeezed lemon juice

Barley is one of the first cultivated grains in history. It is used to brew beer and whiskey and it is the fourth most–grown grain in the world, after corn, rice and wheat. However, most people have never eaten barley in its whole form as a cooked grain. Barley is very nourishing and is rich in minerals and vitamins. It cleans fat and mucus from the body and makes your skin smooth and clean.

For this recipe, I use pearled barley, which is lighter, sweeter and more pleasant in taste. Whole barley can be a little bit heavy. This is a wonderful way to try a forgotten and underestimated grain that should definitely become more mainstream.

METHOD

Pressure cook the pearl barley in 350 ml (12 fl oz) of water, following the instructions on page 69.

Heat the sunflower oil in a heavy-based saucepan (it should reach 4 cm/1½ in up the side of the pan) over high heat until it reaches 180°C (350°F). The oil is ready when two wooden chopsticks dipped into the oil sizzle vigorously around their edges. Deep-fry the seitan for 1–2 minutes, until crisp and golden brown. Drain on paper towel.

Heat the olive oil in a frying pan over medium–high heat. Add the onion and a pinch of salt and sauté for 2–3 minutes, then add the tomato, fried seitan, rocket or turnip greens, garlic, ½ teaspoon of salt and a generous grind of black pepper and sauté for another 2 minutes. Add the pearl barley and sauté for a final 2 minutes until heated through. Finish with the lemon juice and you're good to go. ∎

Rainbow soba noodle salad

~~~~~~~~~

Serves 4
Preparation time: 30 minutes

INGREDIENTS

- 200 g (7 oz) soba noodles
- 3 tablespoons roasted sesame oil
- 1 tablespoon olive oil
- 70 g (2½ oz) cashews
- 1 teaspoon shoyu
- 1 carrot, julienned
- 1 garlic clove, grated
- sea salt
- 1 tablespoon mirin
- 1 long cucumber, deseeded, cut into matchsticks
- 2 oranges, cut into 5 mm (¼ in) thick rounds
- 12 radishes, thinly sliced
- 1 sheet of nori, cut into thin strips
- 50 g (1¾ oz) pickled ginger, cut into matchsticks
- 2 spring onions (scallions), thinly sliced

SOBA NOODLE SAUCE

- 2 tablespoons freshly squeezed lemon juice
- 2 tablespoons shoyu
- 2 tablespoons brown rice vinegar
- 2 tablespoons pure maple syrup
- 1 garlic clove, grated
- 2 cm (¾ in) piece of ginger, peeled and grated

Soba are Japanese noodles made from buckwheat flour. As buckwheat is a very strengthening grain, soba noodles were traditionally eaten to gain physical strength and vitality. In this salad, I use soba to make a light summery dish with colourful toppings. It is full of wonderful textures with a sauce that makes it pop and gives it a Japanese/Asian flair. It is easy to make and you get a joyful party on the plate, which is also a delight for your eyes.

METHOD

Bring 1.5 litres (6 cups) of water to the boil in a saucepan. Add the soba noodles and cook, stirring occasionally with a wooden spoon, for 5 minutes or until al dente. Drain and refresh under cold water — this will prevent the soba noodles sticking together. Return the noodles to the pan, drizzle over 2 tablespoons of the sesame oil and mix to combine.

Heat the olive oil and cashews in a small saucepan over medium heat and roast, stirring often to avoid burning the nuts, for 2 minutes or until golden brown. Transfer the nuts to a small bowl, add the shoyu and stir to coat.

Heat the remaining 1 tablespoon of sesame oil in a frying pan over medium heat. Add the carrot and the garlic and sauté for 2 minutes, then add a pinch of salt and the mirin and sauté for another minute.

Combine the soba noodle sauce ingredients in a small bowl.

Divide the soba noodles among plates and top with a generous amount of the sauce. Top with the carrot, cucumber, orange, radish, nori, pickled ginger, spring onion and cashews and enjoy with chopsticks. ∎

Whole-oat porridge with dried apricots

〜〜〜〜〜

Serves 4
Preparation time: 10 minutes
Wait time: 45 minutes

INGREDIENTS

- 250 g (9 oz) whole oats
- sea salt
- 150 g (5½ oz) dried apricots, halved
- 4 tablespoons brown almond butter (or white almond butter)
- ½ teaspoon ground cinnamon
- ¼ teaspoon vanilla powder
- 60 ml (¼ cup) pure maple syrup
- 1 tablespoon freshly squeezed lemon juice

Porridge is a great meal to eat for breakfast. It will supply you with complex carbohydrates that your body will use as fuel throughout the day. I want to introduce you to making porridges from whole grains. Although oatmeal is relatively healthy, it's still partly processed and therefore not as strengthening as whole oats. Most people, however, are unfamiliar with whole oats and the technique of cooking them is a little more complex. I use a pressure cooker to make the oats softer, creamier and more digestible.

It's important to vary the grains that you're eating on a daily basis, because each grain has its own properties, nutrients and energies. In this recipe, I bring some variation to the grains that you can choose. How exciting is the journey of cooking and discovering this ancient taste of staple foods that have nourished people for thousands of years? When was the last time you cooked with whole oats, whole rye or whole spelt? If you haven't already, do give it a try — I assure you that this morning porridge will give you very steady energy. After eating it, you'll definitely be set to go for your training run, ice-skating or biking activity! These kinds of foods and grains are desperately missing in mainstream plant-based cuisine. They are the most nourishing, the ones that give real core strength to the body — and they're cheap. When we talk about foods of the future, whole grains should be one of the main types. They are energising, sustainable to grow, nutrient dense and inexpensive. If you want to change the world, or you're concerned about sustainability or the health crisis, start eating whole grains on a daily basis. This will be the a first significant step towards the solution.

If you don't have time in the morning, you can pressure cook the grains in advance the night before and then finish the porridge in the morning. Or you can make grains for dinner, which I recommend, and then you'll always have the basis ready for your porridge! Easy!

METHOD

Place the whole oats in a pressure cooker, add 1 litre (4 cups) of water and use your hand to gently rinse the oats. Discard the water and repeat again if necessary until the water runs clear. Add 750 ml (3 cups) of water and a big pinch of salt to the pressure cooker, then cover and secure the pressure cooker lid. Place the pressure cooker over high heat and allow to come to medium pressure. Reduce the heat to low and place the cooker on top of a flame deflector (this will prevent the pressure increasing too much). Cook for 45 minutes, then turn off the heat and allow the pressure to release naturally.

Open the pressure cooker and place over low heat. Add the dried apricots, almond butter, ground cinnamon, vanilla powder and maple syrup and stir to combine. Simmer, covered, for 10 minutes until the porridge is thick and there's a good balance between creaminess and moisture. If the porridge is too thick, add more water; if it's too thin, cook, uncovered, over medium heat until some of the moisture has evaporated. In general, the longer you cook the porridge and the more you stir it, the creamier it will be. If you are in a hurry, 10 minutes will be just fine. Stir through the lemon juice and serve steaming hot. ∎

Sweet rice pilaf with almonds, raisins & cinnamon

Serves 4
Preparation time: 10 minutes
Wait time: 45 minutes

INGREDIENTS

- 2 tablespoons unroasted sesame oil
- 50 g (⅓ cup) raw almonds, thinly sliced
- 50 g (1¾ oz) raisins
- 25 g (1 oz) ground flaxseeds (linseeds)
- 1 teaspoon ground cinnamon
- about 500 g (1 lb 2 oz) left-over cooked brown rice (follow the method for cooking brown rice on page 69)
- 3 tablespoons rice syrup
- 1 tablespoon freshly squeezed lemon juice

When I don't really feel like a meal but would like a snack, I make this dish. I think this was one of the first dishes I used to make after I started to eat a plant-based wholefood diet. It is so simple and so improvised that I was almost ashamed to put it in a cookbook. However, over the years it kept coming back and I never got tired of it. And as many people ask me about a snack they can make, I thought it was time to share this recipe with the world. It's also a great way to use your left-over grains. Snacks, like energy bars, are usually made from nuts and dry fruits and actually are lacking core power. Here I use a whole grain, which means this snack is full of strengthening energy.

METHOD

Heat the sesame oil in a frying pan over medium heat. Add the almonds and sauté, stirring constantly, for about 1 minute, until slightly golden. Add the raisins, ground flaxseeds, cinnamon and the cooked rice and sauté, stirring constantly for 2–3 minutes, until heated through. Stir through the rice syrup and lemon juice and cook for another minute, then divide among plates and serve. ▪

Brown rice with roasted sweet potatoes & dried apricots

〜〜〜〜〜

Serves 4
Preparation time: 20 minutes
Wait time: 45 minutes

INGREDIENTS

- 200 g (7 oz) brown short-grain rice
- 100 g (3½ oz) brown sweet rice
- 1 sweet potato (about 500 g/ 1 lb 2 oz), cut into 1 cm (½ in) thick chunks
- 60 ml (¼ cup) olive oil
- sea salt and black pepper
- ¼ teaspoon pul biber (Aleppo pepper)
- 75 g (2¾ oz) sunflower seeds
- 1 tablespoon roasted sesame oil
- 4 spring onions (scallions), thinly sliced
- 1 garlic clove, finely chopped
- 2 cm (¾ in) piece of ginger, finely chopped
- 125 g (4½ oz) dried apricots, thinly sliced

A colleague of mine who I care about was having a really hard time and I didn't know what to do or say to help her. As a matter of fact, I couldn't do much. So I thought, 'I can cook, that's what I can do'. I wanted to cook something that was sweet, a little bit comforting and would give her some stability at the same time. Brown rice is very strengthening and contributes to a stable mind and mental balance. Sweet potato is always very comforting and creamy. I added extra dried apricots to give it even more sweetness. When I arrived at her place, she couldn't talk, and neither could I. I knew she hadn't eaten anything for days. When I served the dish, she felt uncomfortable about refusing it, because I had made it especially for her. So we ate a little bit, and afterwards we even talked a bit, and this was a small victory. She asked for the recipe and when I got back home I wrote it down. That's the power that food has. It can bring people together. It can comfort you. It can make harder times a bit easier. Life goes up and down. There are more joyful and less joyful days in life, but food is always there. It's there to nourish and support us, and to give an answer, to fill up the gaps that are missing in hard times.

METHOD

Preheat the oven to 180°C (350°F) fan-forced. Pressure cook the rice in 425 ml (14½ fl oz) of water, following the instructions on page 69.

Place the sweet potato on a baking tray, drizzle over 3 tablespoons of the olive oil and sprinkle with ¼ teaspoon of salt, a generous grind of black pepper and the pul biber. Roast in the oven for 30 minutes or until cooked through.

Heat the remaining 1 tablespoon of olive oil in a small saucepan over low heat. Add the sunflower seeds and a pinch of salt and cook for about 5 minutes, until golden brown. Heat the sesame oil in a saucepan over high heat. Add the spring onion, garlic and ginger and sauté for 1 minute.

In a serving bowl, combine the brown rice, sweet potato, sunflower seeds, spring onion mixture and dried apricots, then serve. ∎

Dim sums with spinach, shiitake & seitan

~~~

Makes 24
Preparation time: 75 minutes

INGREDIENTS

- 250 g (1⅔ cups) unbleached plain (all-purpose) flour
- 140 ml (4½ fl oz) just-boiled water

DIM SUM FILLING

- 75 g (2¾ oz) fresh shiitake mushrooms, stems removed, finely chopped
- 50 g (1 cup) spinach, washed and thinly sliced
- 75 g (2¾ oz) seitan, finely chopped
- 1 garlic clove, finely chopped
- 2 cm (¾ in) piece of ginger, peeled and finely chopped
- 2 spring onions (scallions), thinly sliced
- ¼ teaspoon sea salt
- 1 teaspoon roasted sesame oil, plus extra for brushing and pan-frying
- 1 teaspoon shoyu
- 1 teaspoon mirin
- cornflour (cornstarch), for dusting

DIPPING SAUCE

- 2 tablespoons shoyu
- 2 tablespoons brown rice vinegar
- 2 tablespoons mirin
- 2 teaspoons lemon juice
- ½ teaspoon chilli oil (optional)

Dim sum is a type of dumpling that originated in China. In this recipe, I steam the dumplings and I also give you the option to pan-fry them if you want. That extra crunch on the bottom will make them an irresistible bite! It's quite some work to make them, but once you start eating you won't regret a moment of it!

We were making them in the middle of February. It was cold and grey outside, and our dim sums were coming out of the steamer warm and shiny. The room was filled with steam and we found much comfort in these small, tasty bites. 'Excellent!' Anthea remarked while I told nostalgic stories about faraway trips to Asia and wondered when we would be able to get back there. As I took the next round of dim sums out of the steamer, the paper beneath them shimmered like a light feather. This time I fried them in the pan and, as we ate them, the only sound we could hear was the crisp crunch of the dim sums in our mouths.

Dumplings:
Step by step

〜〜〜

PREPARATION

〜〜〜1

To make the dough, place the plain flour in a bowl and add the just-boiled water. Mix very well with a wooden spoon until it comes together into a homogenous dough. It might seem like the mixture is too dry at first, but don't worry because it will come right in the end.

〜〜〜2

〜〜〜2

Knead the dough on an unfloured work surface for about 10 minutes. Return the dough to the bowl and rest, covered with paper towel or a tea towel, for 20–30 minutes.

〜〜〜1

~~~ 3, 4, 5

To make the filling, in a large bowl combine the shiitake mushroom, spinach, seitan, garlic, ginger, spring onion, salt, sesame oil, shoyu and mirin. The mixture will smell amazing!

~~~ 3

~~~ 4

〜〜〜 6

Using a dough scraper or the
back of a large knife, cut the dough
(which will still be slightly warm)
into two equal pieces and roll
each piece on an unfloured work
surface into a long sausage about
3 cm (1¼ in) in diameter.

〜〜〜 6

〜〜〜 7

Cut each sausage into about
12 equal pieces.

〜〜〜 8

Using your fingers, gently stretch
each piece of dough into a small
flat circle.

〜〜〜 7

〜〜〜 8

~~~9

Lightly flour your work surface and a rolling pin with a little cornflour, then roll out the circles of dough until 1 mm (1/32 in) thick. You can stack the wrappers on top of each other, dusted with a little cornflour, and keep them under a damp tea towel to prevent them drying out.

~~~9

~~~10

Place 1 tablespoon of the filling in the centre of each wrapper.

~~~10

~~~ 11, 12, 13, 14, 15

Working with one wrapper at a time, grab the edge of the wrapper and start to make small folds about 1 cm (½ in) deep along the edge of the wrapper, then bring the folds together as shown in the image.

As you keep making the folds, they'll eventually come together to enclose the filling. Pinch the top of the dumpling with your fingers so that it doesn't open upon steaming. And if it does open, it's not the end of the world!

~~~ 11

~~~ 12

~~~ 13

~~~ 14

~~~ 15

〜〜 16, 17, 18

Line a steamer basket with baking paper and poke some holes using a skewer or a toothpick to allow the steam to come through. If you don't have a steamer, you can use a colander set over a large saucepan, but don't forget the baking paper so that the dim sums don't stick. Lightly brush the baking paper with sesame oil to avoid sticking, then place the dim sum in the steamer basket (you may need to work in batches).

〜〜 16

〜〜 17

Bring 5 cm (2 in) of water to the boil in a steamer pan and place the basket on top.

Cover and steam the dim sums for 10–15 minutes, until shiny and slightly transparent.

〜〜 18

〜〜 19

〜〜〜 **19**
Meanwhile, combine the shoyu, brown rice vinegar, mirin, lemon juice and chilli oil (if using) to make the dipping sauce.

〜〜 20

〜〜〜 **20**
You can serve the dim sums steamed or pan-fry them to make them nice and crispy. To pan-fry, heat 2 tablespoons of sesame oil in a frying pan over medium heat. Once the oil is hot, add the dim sums and pan-fry for 3–4 minutes, until crisp and golden brown on the base. The oil needs to be sizzling but the dim sums can easily burn, so watch carefully and adjust the heat accordingly.

Serve the dim sums hot straight from the pan or steamer basket with the dipping sauce on the side. ▪

Quick spaghetti
with shimeji mushrooms

~~~~~~~~~~

Serves 4
Preparation time: 15 minutes

INGREDIENTS

- 250 g (9 oz) spaghetti
- 3 tablespoons olive oil
- 350 g (12½ oz) shimeji mushrooms
- black pepper

I learned this recipe when I was in Fukui Prefecture, Japan. I was invited on this trip by Japanese journalist Yukiko Matsuoka. Years before, when I met her in the Netherlands, she told me that when I came to Japan, I should meet Akihiko Dosaka, a chef in Fukui whose style is very similar to mine.

After years of dreaming of this trip, when I finally stepped into his small quirky little restaurant, Flat Kitchen, I knew it immediately. Feeling the vibes inside this tiny atmospheric bar-restaurant and the smells that came from the kitchen, I thought 'Yes, I can see why it is similar to what I do.' His energy, cooking style, his way of moving in the kitchen and the way he combines tastes in a very indirect way were things I could really recognise. The first dish he served us was this one. Just a simple pasta with shimeji mushrooms. I thought, 'Oh my god, that's almost too simple to be served in a restaurant', but it was delicious and brilliant.

One thing led to another, and we decided to cook a dinner together at his restaurant about a week after our first meeting. We ended up cooking a 10-course menu together, which will always stay in my memory. Cooking in a local small quirky Japanese countryside restaurant? Meeting a professional soulmate halfway across the world? Learning how to make pasta in Japan? (Yes, please, because the Japanese do everything better.)

This trip lives on in my memories but I can keep on making this pasta again and again and reliving that moment in time.

METHOD

Bring 1.5 litres (6 cups) of water and a pinch of salt to the boil in a large saucepan. Add the pasta and cook for 7–8 minutes, until al dente. Drain.

Meanwhile, heat the olive oil in a frying pan or wok over medium heat. Add the mushrooms, ½ teaspoon of salt and a generous grind of black pepper and sauté for 3–4 minutes, until softened. Add the spaghetti and ¼ teaspoon of salt and sauté, stirring, for another 1–2 minutes. Serve immediately and enjoy the simplicity of this dish! ▪

Soba noodles with carrot & ginger tempura in clear Japanese broth

~~~~~~~~~

Serves 4
Preparation time: 20 minutes

INGREDIENTS

- 5 cm (2 in) piece of kombu
- 4 dried shiitake mushrooms
- 1 x 10 g (¼ oz) sachet instant dashi powder
- 2 tablespoons shoyu
- 6 cm (2½ in) piece of ginger, 2 cm (¾ in) grated, 4 cm (1½ in) cut into matchsticks
- 250 g (9 oz) dried soba noodles
- 50 g (⅓ cup) white unbleached plain (all-purpose) flour
- 50 g (1¾ oz) rice flour
- 150 ml (5 fl oz) sparkling water (ideally chilled)
- 1 carrot, julienned
- 500–750 ml (2–3 cups) organic sunflower oil, for deep-frying
- 1 spring onion (scallion), thinly sliced, to serve

Ramen are highly celebrated in the West, but most people are less familiar with the more common and traditional Japanese noodles in a broth. When you stroll through the streets of Japan, you come across many udon and soba snack bars. These are very small restaurants with few seats only, where you can enjoy an amazing bowl of udon noodles or soba noodles in a broth for just a few pennies. You can usually also purchase an enormous tempura of different vegetables but you might feel this tempura in your stomach for a few hours after the meal.

I hope that with the tempura in this recipe, you will gain a different — and lighter — experience. I took the method for this recipe from my macrobiotic teacher Wieke Nelissen. I always admired her simple and elegant way of cooking and reinventing Japanese dishes, but it was only when I travelled to Japan and other places in Asia that I understood how refined her skills were and how deep her knowledge and experience went. This dish is a true pearl. Please try it. It will give you very nice energy.

METHOD

To make the clear Japanese broth, pour 1 litre (4 cups) of water into a saucepan and add the kombu, shiitake mushrooms and dashi powder. Bring to a gentle simmer over low heat and cook for about 15 minutes, until the shiitake have expanded and softened. Remove the mushrooms from the broth, then cut away and discard the stems and thinly slice the mushroom caps. Return the sliced mushrooms to the broth and add the shoyu. Using your hand, squeeze the juice from the grated ginger into the broth and continue to simmer, without boiling, for 2 more minutes. Turn off the heat.

~~~~~~~~~~~~~~~~~~~~~

Bring 1.5 litres (6 cups) of water to the boil and add the soba noodles. The soba noodles already contain salt so there's no need to add salt to the cooking water. The cooking time will depend on the brand of noodles — I usually cook mine for about 3 minutes until very al dente (or according to the packet instructions). Drain the noodles and rinse them in cold water. Set to one side.

To prepare the tempura, place the plain and rice flour and sparkling water in a bowl and mix as little as possible until just combined — it's okay if there are still a few lumps. Add the carrot and ginger and mix to coat.

Heat the oil in a heavy-based saucepan (it should reach 4 cm/1½ in up the side of the pan) over high heat until it reaches 180°C (350°F). The oil is ready when two wooden chopsticks dipped into the oil sizzle vigorously around their edges.

Using your hands or chopsticks, take a thin bundle of batter-covered vegetables and gently lower them into the oil. Fry for 1–2 minutes each side until golden brown. Drain on a plate lined with paper towel and repeat with the remaining battered vegetables.

Divide the soba noodles among shallow soup bowls and pour the broth over the top. Add the tempura and spring onion and serve. Enjoy the crunch of the tempura and slurp the noodles loudly and impolitely. ▪

BASICS: DEEP-FRYING

~~~~

Heat 500–750 ml (2–3 cups) of oil suitable for deep-frying in a heavy-based saucepan over high heat (the oil should reach 4 cm/1½ in up the side of the pan). Heat the oil to 180°C (350°F) or until two wooden chopsticks dipped into the oil sizzle vigorously around their edges. Add your chosen ingredients and deep-fry for 1–3 minutes, until very crisp and golden brown. Remove the ingredients from the oil and drain on paper towel. ▪

Basics: Pressure cooker brown rice

Serves 4
Preparation time: 5 minutes
Cook time: 45 minutes

INGREDIENTS

- 225 g (8 oz) brown short-grain rice
- 75 g (2½ oz) brown sweet rice (or brown short-grain rice if unavailable)
- ¼ teaspoon sea salt

You can also use this recipe to prepare all types of whole grain: brown rice, whole oats, whole rye, barley, farro and spelt. For a soft creamy porridge from any type of grain, use the same recipe with a double amount of water. You can find the recipe for millet on page 185.

If you don't have a pressure cooker, you can use a normal pan to make this recipe. Use 720 ml (24½ fl oz) water and cook the rice for 60–75 minutes, until the rice is soft and sticky and all the water has evaporated.

METHOD

Place both types of rice in a pressure cooker, add enough water to cover and gently use your hand to swirl the rice in the water. Drain and, if necessary, repeat again until the water runs clear.

Drain and return the rice to the pressure cooker. Add 475 ml (16 fl oz) of water and the salt, then close the pressure cooker and bring to medium pressure over high heat. When the cooker reaches pressure, place a flame deflector between the pan and the gas flame, reduce the heat to low and pressure cook the rice for 45 minutes.

Turn off the heat and allow the pressure to release naturally. Open the pressure cooker and stir gently with a wooden spoon, to aerate the rice. If not using immediately, cover the cooker with a bamboo sheet or sushi mat to keep the rice warm. ▪

A big wok of soba noodles

~~~~~~~~~

Serves 4
Preparation time: 15 minutes

INGREDIENTS

- 200 g (7 oz) dried soba noodles
- 3 tablespoons
  roasted sesame oil
- 1 onion, thinly sliced
  into half moons
- 1 carrot, cut into thin matchsticks
- 1 garlic clove, finely chopped
- 4 cm (1½ in) piece
  of ginger, grated
- ¼ teaspoon chilli flakes
- pinch of sea salt
- 200 g (7 oz) broccolini, thick
  stalks cut in half lengthways
- 5 spring onions (scallions),
  thinly sliced
- 3 tablespoons mirin
- 1 tablespoon pure maple syrup
- 3 tablespoons shoyu
- 1 tablespoon brown rice vinegar

Soba noodles are made of buckwheat flour, which is traditionally used to give strength and energy. In this recipe, I sauté them with other vegetables. This is a light and dynamic way to prepare them. This dish is very easy to make, and can be ready in 20 minutes. It will definitely satisfy your craving for real, warm Asian street food. There are no excuses for not cooking.

METHOD

Bring 1.5 litres (6 cups) of water to the boil in a large saucepan and add the soba noodles. The soba noodles already contain salt so there's no need to add salt to the cooking water. Boil the noodles for 5–6 minutes until al dente, then drain and rinse the noodles under cold water.

Heat the sesame oil in a frying pan or wok over medium–high heat. Add the onion, carrot, garlic, ginger, chilli flakes and salt and sauté for 2–3 minutes. Add the broccolini and sauté for 1 minute, then add the cooked noodles and sauté for another 3–4 minutes. Add the spring onion, mirin, maple syrup, shoyu and brown rice vinegar and sauté for another 3 minutes. Divide among bowls and eat steaming hot. ▪

BEANS &

PROTEINS

Beans & proteins

~~~~

Legumes or pulses, commonly called beans, are the seeds of the flowering plants of the *Fabaceae* family. This group includes chickpeas, lentils, peas and all types of beans, including red beans, adzuki beans white, black beans, soy beans, broad beans and many more. Beans are a very rich source of protein and, together with whole grains, form the main source of protein in plant-based cuisine. Beans are also rich in fibre, and minerals such as iron, calcium, magnesium and phosphorous as well as other minerals and vitamins. Energetically speaking, beans provide deep down strength to the whole body. In Chinese traditional medicine, they nourish the kidneys, bladder and sexual organs (both male and female). These organs are responsible for courage, deeper strength, endurance and confidence.

Beans are used worldwide in all traditional cuisines. They have been our main source of protein, certainly since the agricultural revolution 12,000 years ago, but also before then, when nomadic societies collected them in the wild. Every culture has its own special dishes that are prepared with beans every day. Often these dishes are combined with grains, making a complete protein. Black beans are used in Mexico, pinto beans in Brazil, adzuki beans in Japan, chickpeas in the Middle East, lentils in the Middle East, India and Africa, and green peas in north-west Europe, just to name a few known examples.

Unfortunately, many families following a modern Western lifestyle have abandoned cooking and eating beans on a daily basis. This is unfortunate, not only because beans are highly nutritious, cheap and sustainable, but also in regard to the benefits of eating a more plant-based diet. Many people who are transitioning to a plant-based diet hope to substitute animal protein with artificial, highly processed meat substitutes, which are becoming more popular and are available in every supermarket. These substitutes are harmful for our digestive system and do not supply our body with the nutrients, fibre, strength and energy we get from wholefoods.

The most straightforward way to transition into a plant-based diet is to avoid falling into the trap of these fake synthetic substitutes (such as vegan hamburgers, vegan milks and vegan yoghurts). Instead, incorporate grains and beans into your daily eating pattern and cooking routine. Although it can be challenging to incorporate beans into your daily cooking routine, try discovering dishes that you can make with beans, and that you will like; which will help beans become part of your cooking repertoire. This is a crucial step in adopting a more plant-based diet. Incorporating beans (alongside grains and vegetables) into your daily eating routine is the only straightforward way into a more plant-based lifestyle. ▪

A stew of white beans with koya dofu & sweet potatoes

Serves 4
Preparation time: 25 minutes
Wait time: 90 minutes (60 minutes if using soaked beans)

INGREDIENTS

- 200 g (7 oz) small or medium-sized dried white beans (optional: soaked overnight in cold water, drained)
- 3 pieces (about 50 g/1¾ oz) koya dofu (freeze-dried tofu)
- 500–750 ml (2–3 cups) organic sunflower oil, for deep-frying
- 2 tablespoons olive oil
- 1 onion, diced
- 1 sweet potato, diced
- 1 bay leaf
- 1 garlic clove, finely grated
- 1 teaspoon ground cumin
- black pepper
- ½ teaspoon sea salt
- chopped parsley, to serve (optional)

This stew is simple, mild and very comforting. I recommend it if you're just starting with beans and need to be convinced how good they taste when they are cooked properly. If you can't find koya dofu, you can use smoked tofu instead.

METHOD

Pressure cook the beans in 700 ml (23½ fl oz) of water, following the instructions on page 102.

Meanwhile, soak the koya dofu in 350 ml (12 fl oz) of water for about 5 minutes or until soft. Drain and squeeze the excess liquid from the koya dofu. Cut into 1 cm (½ in) cubes.

Heat the sunflower oil in a heavy-based saucepan (it should reach 4 cm/1½ in up the side of the pan) over high heat until it reaches 180°C (350°F). The oil is ready when two wooden chopsticks dipped into the oil sizzle vigorously around their edges. Add the koya dofu and deep-fry for 1 minute until a little crisp. Drain on a plate lined with paper towel.

Heat the olive oil in a flameproof casserole dish (Dutch oven) over medium–high heat. Add the onion, sweet potato and bay leaf and sauté for 10 minutes until just tender and slightly golden. Add the garlic, cumin and a generous grind of black pepper and sauté for another 2–3 minutes. If the base of the pan starts to dry out, add a tablespoon of water.

Add the beans and their cooking water, the koya dofu and salt and bring to the boil. Reduce the heat to medium, then cover and simmer for 15 minutes or until the vegetables are tender. Serve with some parsley scattered over the top (if using) and savour this comforting dish. ▪

Broad bean salad with harissa & preserved lemon from Keren Rubenstein

Serves 4
Preparation time: 15 minutes

INGREDIENTS

- ½ teaspoon sea salt
- 1.5 kg (3 lb 5 oz) fresh broad (fava) beans, podded (to yield 500 g/1 lb 2 oz beans)
- 15 g (½ oz) coriander (cilantro) leaves and stalks, finely chopped
- 85 g (3 oz) preserved lemon, skin and flesh roughly chopped (reserve any pickling liquid)
- 3 tablespoons freshly squeezed lemon juice
- 1 tablespoon Harissa (see page 83)
- 2 tablespoons olive oil
- black pepper
- sourdough bread or challah, to serve

Keren Rubenstein is a dear friend and without doubt the best cook in Amsterdam. I always ask her, 'How can I make these amazing desserts like you make but without sugar, eggs and butter?'. She looks at me questioningly, so I say, 'OK, let's go into the kitchen, peel some broad beans and talk about how to preserve lemons and which is the best harissa in town'.

We meet on the crossroad between my healthy, clean vegan style of cooking and her very rich food that she makes with animal products and sugar. We meet on the crossroad between her kitchen and mine in the smallest, messiest and greatest kitchen in town (hers!). This is where we both feel more comfortable.

Keren told me that her father used to make this salad for every Shabbat dinner. I looked at her with wonder and tried to figure out her secrets for cooking. How does she do it? When we taste the salad, we are both amazed at the explosion of the flavours from the harissa and the preserved lemons, and how the elegance of the broad beans brings these flavours together.

She also said that this salad goes well with sourdough bread or challah (Jewish bread). I listen and feel almost uncomfortable to ask her to teach me how to make these as well. This salad is a great example of Keren's unique talent and ability to make food that stays with you, bringing memories, stories and love for people. I feel very lucky to be able to share it with you here.

Keren is one of the most inspiring and generous people I know. If you haven't tried her food, you definitely should. You can follow her on her Instagram page (@kerenruben), her blog (kerenruben.com) or join her robust and buzzing foodie Facebook group (Amsterdam cooks)where Keren welcomes people from the whole world and makes everyone feel immediately at home, just like she always does.

METHOD

Bring 1.5 litres (6 cups) of water and the salt to the boil in a large saucepan over high heat. Add the broad beans, then reduce the heat to medium, cover and cook for 5–6 minutes, until the beans are very soft — they should maintain their shape, but mash easily when pressed between two fingers. You will know the beans are ready because they will turn bright green under their skins. Drain the beans and transfer to a salad bowl and allow to cool to room temperature.

Add the coriander, preserved lemon (and any pickling liquid from the lemon), lemon juice, harissa, olive oil and a generous grind of black pepper and toss to combine. Eat with a slice of comforting sourdough bread or challah. ▪

Basics:
Harissa

Makes 250 g (9 oz)
Preparation time: 10 minutes
Wait time: 30 minutes

INGREDIENTS

- 4 red sweet-pointed capsicums (peppers)
- 15 cherry tomatoes
- 1 garlic clove
- ¼ teaspoon ground cumin
- ¼ teaspoon ground coriander
- ½ teaspoon sea salt
- ⅛ teaspoon chilli flakes
- ½ teaspoon pul biber (Aleppo pepper)
- 2 tablespoons olive oil

Harissa is a thick and spicy Tunisian sauce made with red bell pepper (capsicum), which gives a real upgrade to your cooking. The colour is gorgeous and the sauce is sensual and flavourful. You can use it as a spread for bread or add it when you roast vegetables in the oven, to give them more flair.

METHOD

Preheat the oven to 180°C (350°F) fan-forced.

Line a baking tray with baking paper.

Place the capsicums and cherry tomatoes on the prepared tray and bake for 30 minutes or until the edges of the vegetables are dark golden. Remove from the oven and set aside to cool, then deseed the capsicums.

Place the capsicum and cherry tomatoes in the bowl of a food processor, along with the remaining ingredients and process until smooth.

Any left-over harissa will keep in a glass jar in the fridge for up to 1 week. ∎

Black bean stew with pumpkin & fried seitan

~~~~~~~~~

Serves 4
Preparation time: 25 minutes
Waiting time: 105 minutes (75 minutes if using soaked beans)

INGREDIENTS

- 200 g (7 oz) dried black beans (optional: soaked overnight in cold water, drained)
- 60 ml (¼ cup) olive oil
- 2 onions, cut into chunks
- 1 kg (2 lb 3 oz) orange Hokkaido pumpkin, cut into big chunks
- 2 garlic cloves, grated
- 2 bay leaves
- 1 teaspoon ground cumin
- ½ teaspoon chilli flakes
- 1 teaspoon sea salt
- black pepper
- 1 teaspoon umesu
- 1 teaspoon shoyu
- 750 ml (3 cups) organic sunflower oil, for deep-frying
- 500 g (1 lb 2 oz) seitan, cut into rough chunks
- 50 g (⅓ cup) plain unbleached (all-purpose) flour
- coriander (cilantro) leaves, to serve

This is a great stew for people who want to eat big, satisfying, filling and strengthening meals. One day a little bird whispered to me that a few dancers and acrobats were coming to my next cooking class. I knew I had to make a dish that would give them a lot of power and energy. I also wanted to show them how fierce plant-based cuisine can be and convince them to come back to my classes. This black bean stew is thick and dominant and, together with the fried seitan, it really makes a protein-rich, energising dish. It's a great dish for winter, but also for when you are physically active and need an extra push. The dancers and acrobats came back to the next class, brought their friends, and the room was filled with testosterone.

METHOD

Pressure cook the beans in 700 ml (23½ fl oz) of water, following the instructions on page 102.

Meanwhile, heat the olive oil in a saucepan over medium–high heat. Add the onion and pumpkin and sauté for 2–3 minutes, until glistening and golden brown. Add the garlic, bay leaves, cumin, chilli flakes, salt and a generous grind of black pepper and sauté for another 2–3 minutes. Add the cooked beans, along with their cooking liquid, then stir through the umesu and shoyu and simmer for 20–30 minutes, until the vegetables are tender. There should always be at least 1 cm (½ in) of liquid in the pan; so add a little water if the pan starts to dry out.

Heat the sunflower oil in a heavy-based saucepan (it should reach 4 cm/1½ in up the side of the pan) over high heat until it reaches 180°C (350°F). The oil is ready when two wooden chopsticks dipped into the oil sizzle vigorously around their edges. Toss the seitan through the flour, then deep-fry for 1–2 minutes, until crisp. Drain on paper towel.

Divide the black bean stew among bowls, top with the deep-fried seitan and a few coriander leaves and serve. ▪

Tempeh wraps with tahini & gherkin

Serves 4
Preparation time: 20 minutes

INGREDIENTS

- 300 g (10½ oz) tempeh, thinly sliced
- 750 ml (3 cups) organic sunflower oil, for deep-frying
- 2 tablespoons shoyu
- 3 tablespoons rice syrup
- 1 teaspoon freshly squeezed lemon juice
- ¼ teaspoon nanami (shichimi) togarashi
- 75 ml (2½ fl oz) olive oil
- 1 carrot, julienned
- sea salt and black pepper
- 50 g (1¾ oz) hulled (white) tahini
- 1 teaspoon freshly squeezed lemon
- 4 wheat flour tortillas
- ¼ lettuce of your choice, leaves separated
- 4 gherkins (pickled cucumbers), thinly sliced
- 1 red onion, finely chopped

This is a very satisfying wrap with a very good taste. Tempeh is an Indonesian fermented soybean cake. I like to deep-fry it to give it a good bite, and I use a strong marinade like the one in this recipe. For the rest of the wrap, I use a combination of Israeli flavours, such as tahini, red onion and gherkin. This will taste like real Israeli street food. It will satisfy your cravings when you feel like a bite of quick, satisfying, uncompromised street food.

METHOD

Deep-fry the tempeh in the sunflower oil according to the instructions on page 68 for 3–4 minutes, until crisp and golden brown.

Transfer the tempeh to a bowl, add the shoyu, rice syrup, lemon juice and nanami togarashi and toss to combine. Set aside.

Heat 1 tablespoon of the olive oil in a frying pan over medium–high heat. Add the carrot and a little salt and pepper and sauté for 3–4 minutes, until the carrot is soft and starting to caramelise.

In a bowl, whisk the tahini, ¼ teaspoon of sea salt, the lemon juice and 40 ml (1¼ fl oz) of water until smooth — it should have the consistency of mayonnaise. If it's too thick, add a little more water and whisk; if it's too thin, add a little more tahini and whisk. Repeat if necessary.

Heat 1 tablespoon of the remaining olive oil in a frying pan over medium–low heat. Add a tortilla and toast for about 1 minute each side until lightly golden. Don't allow the tortilla to become crisp or it will break when you roll it into a wrap. Repeat with the remaining 3 tablespoons of olive oil and tortillas.

Spread the tahini sauce over each tortilla and top with the lettuce, tempeh, carrot, gherkin and red onion, placed slightly off centre. Roll up the tortillas and get stuck in. ▪

Chilli sin carne with kidney beans, guacamole & fried tortilla chips

Serves 4
Preparation time: 45 minutes
Wait time: 105 minutes (75 minutes if using soaked beans)

INGREDIENTS

- 200 g (1 cup) kidney beans (optional: soaked overnight in cold water, drained)
- 3 tablespoons olive oil
- 2 red onions, thinly sliced into half moons
- 2 carrots, grated
- 2 red sweet-pointed capsicums (peppers), thinly sliced
- 2 teaspoons sea salt
- black pepper
- 4 garlic cloves, finely chopped
- ½ teaspoon smoked paprika
- 1 sprig of oregano
- ½ teaspoon chopped chipotle pepper (or chipotle paste)
- 2 x 400 g (14 oz) tins peeled tomatoes
- 1 teaspoon tomato purée (concentrated purée)
- 1 tablespoon shoyu
- 1 tablespoon pure maple syrup

SPICED TEMPEH

- 500–750 ml (2–3 cups) organic sunflower oil, for deep-frying
- 300 g (10½ oz) tempeh, thinly sliced
- 2 tablespoons shoyu
- 3 tablespoons rice syrup
- 1 teaspoon freshly squeezed lemon juice
- ¼ teaspoon nanami (shichimi) togarashi

This is a massively protein-rich dish that any carnivore will love to eat. The kidney bean chilli is rich, thick and filling. The tempeh is crisp and spicy — some people tell me it tastes like bacon (I am not sure what bacon tastes like, but I will take their word for it). The guacamole is a dream. Be careful not to eat all the tortilla chips before the dish is served!

METHOD

Pressure cook the kidney beans in 700 ml (23½ fl oz) of water, following the instructions on page 102. Drain and discard the cooking water.

Heat the olive oil in a flameproof casserole dish (Dutch oven) over medium heat. Add the onion, carrot and capsicum and sauté for 6–7 minutes, until the vegetables are soft. Add the salt, a generous grind of black pepper, the garlic, smoked paprika, oregano and chipotle pepper and sauté for another 5 minutes. Add a tablespoon of water if the base of the dish starts to dry out.

Add the drained kidney beans, tomatoes, tomato purée, shoyu and maple syrup and bring to the boil. Reduce the heat to low and cook for 30 minutes or until the beans and vegetables are soft.

For the tempeh, heat the oil in a heavy-based saucepan (it should reach 4 cm/1½ in up the side of the pan) over high heat until it reaches 180°C (350°F). The oil is ready when two wooden chopsticks dipped into the oil sizzle vigorously around their edges. Deep-fry the tempeh for 3–4 minutes, until crisp and golden brown. Drain on paper towel, then transfer to a bowl, along with the shoyu, rice syrup, lemon juice and nanami togarashi and toss to combine.

TORTILLA CHIPS

- 2–4 wheat flour tortillas
- sea salt

GUACAMOLE

- 1 avocado
- 1 teaspoon freshly
  squeezed lime juice
- ¼ teaspoon sea salt
- black pepper
- ½ garlic clove, grated
- ½ red onion, finely chopped
- 1 teaspoon olive oil
- 10 cherry tomatoes, diced
- 2 cm (¾ in) long red chilli,
  finely chopped

TO SERVE

- finely chopped red onion
- coriander (cilantro) leaves

Bring the oil back to a temperature of 180°C (350°F). Tear the tortillas into rough pieces, then lower into the oil and deep-fry for 1–2 minutes, until golden brown. Drain on paper towel and sprinkle with a generous amount of salt.

To make the guacamole, in a bowl, mash together the avocado and lime juice. Add the salt, some black pepper, the garlic, red onion, olive oil, cherry tomato and red chilli and mix well.

Serve big bowls of the hot chilli sin carne topped with the crispy tempeh, guacamole and tortilla chips. Garnish with a little red onion and a few coriander leaves. ▪

How to
aid digestion

Many people have problems digesting beans, and complain
about gas forming. Here are a few tips to deal with this problem.

1
As you advance into eating a wholefoods plant-
based diet, your guts will get more used to eating
them and will develop enzymes to digest beans
and grains.

2
Avoid eating any dairy foods. The combination
of dairy foods and beans can produce a lot of
acid in your guts.

3
Start by eating small quantities of beans (you
don't need much) and chew them very well.
Chewing increases your digestive enzymes
and helps digestion enormously.

4
Maintain a general good balance in your diet. When
a plate has a variety of foods, like sea vegetables,
pickles and various vegetables, you will be able to
digest a small portion of beans more easily.

5
Soak the beans overnight before cooking them, and
discard the soaking water. The soaking water contains
acids from the beans, which are harder to digest.

6 〜〜〜
Pressure cook the beans. This makes them softer, more digestible and allows your intestines to absorb more nutrients from the beans. Pressure cooking also makes the beans creamier, softer and tastier.

7 〜〜〜
Add kombu to the cooking water. Kombu is a type of seaweed that is very rich in minerals. It helps balance the acids that are more difficult to digest, and adds more minerals to the beans and their cooking water. You'll need a piece about 5 cm (2 in) long when you cook beans for 4 people. ▪

Jerusalem salad

Serves 4
Preparation time: 15 minutes
Wait time: 75 minutes (45 minutes if using soaked chickpeas)

INGREDIENTS

- 200 g (7 oz) dried chickpeas (garbanzo beans) (optional: soaked overnight in cold water, drained)
- 500–750 ml (2–3 cups) organic sunflower oil, for deep-frying
- 100 g (3½ oz) bread, cut into small cubes
- 1 red onion, finely chopped
- 35 g (1¼ oz) parsley, finely chopped
- 1 long cucumber, deseeded, finely chopped
- 350 g (12½ oz) tomatoes or cherry tomatoes, finely chopped
- 200 g (1 cup) sweetcorn kernels
- 200 g (7 oz) feto (fermented tofu), crumbled
- 1 teaspoon sea salt
- black pepper
- 2 tablespoons freshly squeezed lemon juice

TAHINI DRESSING

- 150 g (5½ oz) hulled (white) tahini
- 2 teaspoons freshly squeezed lemon juice
- ½ teaspoon sea salt

There are many versions of this salad. It's based on typical Middle Eastern Israeli/Arabic ingredients. It is not necessarily traditional — this is my modern version of it. You will typically find this kind of salad in street stalls or bistros, where you can eat it as a quick lunch. Its lightness makes it very suitable for lunch and for warmer days. At the same time, it is still filling so people often eat it as a main dish. I recommend you (pressure) cook the chickpeas yourself, but if you are short on time and want to make it quickly, you could use chickpeas from a jar or tin.

METHOD

Pressure cook the chickpeas in 700 ml (23½ fl oz) of water, following the instructions on page 102.

Meanwhile, heat the oil in a heavy-based saucepan (it should reach 4 cm/1½ in up the side of the pan) over high heat until it reaches 180°C (350°F). The oil is ready when two wooden chopsticks dipped into the oil sizzle vigorously around their edges. Add the bread cubes and deep-fry for 1–2 minutes, until crisp and golden brown. Drain on paper towel.

You can also make the croutons in a preheated 180°C (350°C) fan-forced oven. Place the bread cubes on a baking tray, drizzle with 3 tablespoons of olive oil and sprinkle with 2 big pinches of salt. Transfer to the oven and bake for 10 minutes, then turn over and continue to bake for 5–10 minutes, until golden and crisp. Set aside to cool.

To make the tahini dressing, combine the tahini, lemon juice, salt and 50 ml (1¾ fl oz) of water in a small bowl and whisk to a thin yoghurt-like texture, adding more water if necessary.

In a salad bowl, combine the chickpeas, croutons, onion, parsley, cucumber, tomato, sweetcorn, feto, salt, a generous grind of black pepper and the lemon juice.

Serve the salad topped with the tahini dressing and imagine you're on holiday in Jerusalem. ∎

Seitan wraps with oyster mushrooms & sundried tomato pesto

Serves 4
Preparation time: 15 minutes

INGREDIENTS

- 500–750 ml (2–3 cups) organic sunflower oil, for deep-frying
- 250 g (9 oz) seitan, cut into chunks
- 90 ml (3 fl oz) olive oil
- 200 g (7 oz) oyster mushrooms
- sea salt and black pepper
- 4 wheat flour tortillas
- 4 teaspoons sundried tomato pesto
- 100 g (3½ oz) turnip (or daikon/kohlrabi/radish), thinly sliced
- 15 g (½ oz) dill fronds
- 100 g (3½ oz) gherkins (pickled cucumbers), thinly sliced

This is a very satisfying and umami-full wrap that I love making for my nephew. Teenagers (but not only them) often crave something that doesn't taste too healthy and green, for example, something they can buy in a shawarma stall. Over the years, I learned to make good-quality food with ingredients that will also be enjoyable for young people who crave junk food almost daily. While satisfying their wild cravings, I can also calm my concerns about their health and what they put in their body.

METHOD

Heat the sunflower oil in a heavy-based saucepan (it should reach 4 cm/1½ in up the side of the pan) over high heat until it reaches 180°C (350°F). The oil is ready when two wooden chopsticks dipped into the oil sizzle vigorously around their edges. Deep-fry the seitan for 1 minute or until golden brown. Drain on paper towel.

Heat 2 tablespoons of the olive oil in a chargrill pan over medium–high heat. Add the mushrooms and cook, undisturbed, for 2 minutes. Turn the mushrooms over, season generously with salt and pepper and sauté for another 2–3 minutes, until the mushrooms are just tender and charred. Remove from the heat.

Heat 1 tablespoon of the remaining olive oil in a frying pan over medium heat. Add a tortilla and toast for about 1 minute each side until lightly golden. Don't allow the tortilla to become crisp or it will break when you roll it into a wrap. Repeat with the remaining 3 tablespoons of olive oil and tortillas.

Spread the pesto over the tortillas and top with the turnip, seitan, mushroom, dill and gherkins. Roll up the wraps and serve warm. ∎

Creamy pasta with pumpkin sauce & white beans topped with almond pesto

Serves 4
Preparation time: 25 minutes
Wait time: 75 mins (45 mins if using soaked beans)

INGREDIENTS

- 225 g (8 oz) white beans (optional: soaked in cold water overnight, drained)
- 1 kg (2 lb 3 oz) yellow or orange Hokkaido pumpkin, unpeeled, cut into big chunks
- 105 ml (3½ fl oz) olive oil
- ½ teaspoon coarse sea salt
- black pepper
- 350 g (12½ oz) spaghetti
- 2 garlic cloves, grated
- 2½ teaspoons sea salt

ALMOND PESTO

- 60 g (⅔ cup) almond flakes
- 80 g (2¾ oz) basil leaves
- 2 garlic cloves, sliced
- zest of 1 lemon
- 1 tablespoon freshly squeezed lemon juice
- 100 ml (3½ fl oz) olive oil
- ½ teaspoon sea salt
- black pepper

This dish is the ultimate comfort food — pasta cooked softly in a creamy pumpkin sauce and tender white beans. In this recipe, the beans, the pumpkin puree and the pasta are cooked together in one big pan, which makes it extra yummy and very cosy.

I learned this recipe from one of my favourite cooks, Mercedes Leon, a Cuban-American plant-based chef who lives in the Netherlands. When it's late and quiet at night, Mercedes' kitchen is where I crave to be and I secretly plan my next visit to come and eat her food. I love stepping into her huge kitchen and sitting at the vast industrial metal countertop on a high bar chair. Mercedes cooks for you with passion and quick movements and as you watch her, she tells you stories about far continents, new tastes and undiscovered cultures. You'll find yourself hearing political discussions, anecdotes about unusual people and tips about impressive cookbooks that you've never heard of before. As you are being enchanted by all this, the meal will be ready and out of politeness you'll have to stop yourself from devouring it at once.

Mercedes' food warms you and gives you an encouraging hug. It is made with big strokes and served on rustic tables for big groups of people who are laughing, debating and playing joyful music. It is food for nomadic groups of flamboyant artists who need a place to crash for the night, before they head to their next adventure in their unknown journey. Mercedes' food is made from the heart. This dish is a perfect example of this — and of so much more.

METHOD

Preheat the oven to 180°C (350°F) fan-forced.

Pressure cook the beans in 700 ml (23½ fl oz) of water, following the instructions on page 102.

~~~~~~~~~~~~~~~~~~~~~~~~~~~~~

Meanwhile, place the pumpkin on a baking tray and drizzle over 60 ml (¼ cup) of the olive oil. Sprinkle with the coarse sea salt and a generous grind of black pepper, then transfer to the oven and roast for 30 minutes or until soft. Place in a bowl and purée with a stick blender until smooth.

Bring 1.2 litres (41 fl oz) of water to the boil in a large saucepan. Add the spaghetti, the beans and their cooking liquid, the pumpkin purée, garlic, sea salt, remaining 3 tablespoons of olive oil and a very generous grind of black pepper. Cook, uncovered and stirring occasionally, for 7–8 minutes, until the pasta is al dente.

Meanwhile, to prepare the pesto, toast the almond flakes in a saucepan over medium heat for 2 minutes, stirring constantly to ensure they don't burn and reducing the heat if necessary. Immediately transfer to a bowl and allow to cool.

Combine the toasted almond flakes, basil, garlic, lemon zest and juice, olive oil, salt and a generous grind of black pepper in a blender or food processor and blend or process to a paste. Divide the pasta among shallow bowls and serve topped with a generous dollop of the pesto. ▪

BASICS: BEANS

**200–250 g (7–9 oz) dried beans
(optional: soaked overnight in cold water, drained)**

~~~~~

Place the beans in a pressure cooker, cover with water and rinse lightly, then drain and return the beans to the pressure cooker. Add 700 ml (23½ fl oz) of water, close the pressure cooker and bring to medium pressure over high heat. When the cooker reaches pressure, place a flame deflector between the pan and the gas flame, then reduce the heat to low and pressure cook the beans for 1 hour 15 minutes for unsoaked beans and 45 minutes for beans soaked overnight. If the pressure increases too much during cooking, reduce the flame to the lowest heat possible or turn it off for 2–3 minutes. Allow the pressure to release naturally. Keep the cooking water to use in stews or soups. ▪

How to cook beans

~~~~

It takes a while to master how to cook beans so that they are tasty, attractive to eat and digestible. I hope the information in this book helps you quickly become familiar with these techniques and that you will soon enjoy cooking your own beans from scratch. I am a big proponent of using a pressure cooker for cooking beans; it is the traditional method in many countries. Avoid using salt, especially at the first stage of the cooking, as this makes them hard and indigestible.

I have included the cooking times for beans when a pressure cooker is not available. Here is a basic guide to cooking beans:

COOKING TIME FOR BEANS

Type of bean	Pressure cooker		Normal pot	
	After soaking overnight	Without soaking	After soaking overnight	Without soaking
chickpeas (garbanzo beans), white beans, black beans, kidney beans, brown beans, broad (fava) beans	45 min	75 min	120 min	Mission impossible
adzuki beans, split peas	15 min	30 min	60 min	90 min
lentils (black, green or brown)	10 min	15 min	20 min	40 min

Note: The hardness of dry beans differs from harvest to harvest and the age of the beans. The cooking time may be longer or shorter than listed in the table above. Use this table as a general indication, but also get to know the beans that you are buying and cooking. If they are too hard, cook them for longer. If they are too soft, cook them a bit less next time.

Other sources of protein

~~~

As well as beans, there are a few products made from beans or grains that I recommend you incorporate in your diet on a daily basis. They will provide you with extra protein and also extra energy. These are naturally and traditionally processed products that you could potentially prepare yourself at home. They differ from commercial meat substitutes in the quality of preparation, nutrition and the energy they supply the body with. They are based on traditional methods of processing food and are not far removed from their whole, original form. They supply the body with proper nutrition and strength and give it a boost of energy.

TOFU

Tofu is a type of a soft 'cheese'. It has a neutral taste and a texture that is similar to mozzarella. Tofu is made by boiling soybeans (the cooking liquid from soybeans is the traditional form of soy milk). The cooking liquid is mixed with nigari, which is a mineral that firms the liquid. The firming material (curd) is pressed into what will later form into a firm block of tofu.

Tofu is a great source of protein and fat, although many people think it is tasteless and lacks character and oomph. I advise you to learn how to make it properly — this will really help you realise tofu can be a delicious treat. In this cookbook, I provide many techniques and recipes for tofu. I hope you try them and start to like tofu as much as I do.

Tofu, in comparison to the other foods in this chapter, lacks energy, strength and compactness. It is a great complementary food, but should never replace beans in your diet. If you only eat tofu on a daily basis without other strengthening foods next to it, you will become more relaxed, round, soft and eventually lack strength and power. Men who eat excessive amounts of tofu and no beans lose their male potential and sexual libido. This is why tofu was often served as daily temple food for male monks in traditional Buddhist temples. Tofu is very diverse. Not only can you make a great variety of dishes with it, you can also find many variations on the product itself. In this cookbook, tofu (unless indicated otherwise) refers to firm tofu. The other varieties that you will see in this book are silken tofu and koya dofu.

SILKEN TOFU

Silken tofu is made with less nigari, so it is softer. It suits dishes with a creamy texture, like cakes, quiches and mousses. You can find it in all organic food stores and Asian supermarkets.

KOYA DOFU

Koya dofu is not easy to find but is well worth searching for (see 'Shops & online stores' on page 291). Koya dofu is traditionally made in the snowy mountains of Japan. It is dried in the sun and freezes at night. This gives koya dofu its special spongy texture. Most people love it because it has a very satisfying bite.

TEMPEH

Tempeh is also a type of 'cheese' made from soybeans. The soybeans are steamed or cooked, inoculated with a fungus called *Rhizopus oligosporus* and fermented for 48 hours.

When the fungus creates mycelia (fluffy white threads), the soybeans are bound into one piece of cheese-like product. Tempeh is firmer than tofu, and it is more strengthening because the whole beans are used in the fermentation process. Tempeh is made traditionally in Indonesia, where it is fermented between banana leaves that naturally contain the *Rhizopus oligosporus* fungus. Tempeh is very nutritious and nourishing and, when prepared properly, can be very satisfying and tasty.

SEITAN

Seitan is not made from beans but from wheat flour, so it is actually a grain product. I have included it in this chapter because it is so rich in protein. Seitan is made by mixing flour and water into an elastic piece of dough, then kneading the piece of dough alternately in hot or cold water to extract the protein (gluten) of the wheat and remove the starch. The piece of gluten that remains is cooked for 20 minutes in a flavourful broth and then it is ready to use. Homemade seitan is much better than the seitan you find in shops, so if you are interested and have the patience, please try to make it yourself. To many people, the texture of seitan reminds them of meat or chicken. I think this comparison is offensive to really good seitan. It is a traditional food that has been prepared in traditional Chinese monasteries and is delicious in its own right.

Only when we learn as a society to use these plant-based sources of proteins in our daily diets, and stop relying on animal-based and synthetic meat substitutes, will we be able to transition into a healthier, more sustainable and ethical lifestyle that will benefit the environment, the animals and ourselves. ▪

Lentil stew with roasted oyster mushrooms, samphire & panko-fried seitan

Serves 4
Preparation time: 25 minutes
Wait time: 1 hour

INGREDIENTS

- 250 g (9 oz) Le Puy green lentils
- sea salt
- 2 teaspoons shoyu
- 2 teaspoons umesu
- 1 teaspoon ground cumin
- 1 tablespoon freshly squeezed lemon juice
- 1 bay leaf
- black pepper
- 60 ml (¼ cup) olive oil
- 400 g (14 oz) cherry tomatoes
- 2 sprigs of rosemary, leaves picked
- ¼ teaspoon coarse sea salt
- 50 g (1¾ oz) samphire
- 4 large oyster mushrooms, cut lengthways into 5 mm (¼ in) thick slices
- 500–750 ml (2–3 cups) organic sunflower oil, for deep-frying
- 40 g (1½ oz) plain unbleached (all-purpose) flour
- 50 g (1¾ oz) panko breadcrumbs
- 200 g (7 oz) seitan, cut into big chunks
- dill fronds or herb of your choice, to serve

Because this recipe is protein-rich and very satisfying, you can make it when you invite several people over. There are quite a few elements in it. Each one is simple on its own but it will take you some time to make all of them.

METHOD

Place the lentils in a saucepan, cover with water and lightly wash. Drain and return the lentils to the pan, along with 550 ml (18½ fl oz) of water and bring to the boil over medium heat. Reduce the heat to a simmer and cook for 45 minutes or until the lentils are just cooked. Add ½ teaspoon of salt, the shoyu, umesu, ground cumin, lemon juice, bay leaf and a generous grind of black pepper and simmer for another 15 minutes. There should always be some liquid in the pan, so top it up if needed.

Meanwhile, heat 2 tablespoons of the olive oil in a frying pan over medium heat. Add the cherry tomatoes, rosemary leaves, coarse sea salt and a generous grind of black pepper and sauté for 2 minutes. Add the samphire and sauté for another minute, then remove from the heat and set aside.

Heat the remaining 2 tablespoons of olive oil in a chargrill pan or frying pan over high heat. Working in batches, add the mushrooms and sauté for 3 minutes each side, until golden with char marks (if using a chargrill pan). After turning, sprinkle generously with salt and pepper. Remove from the heat and set aside.

Heat the sunflower oil in a heavy-based saucepan (it should reach 4 cm/1½ in up the side) over high heat until it reaches 180°C (350°F).

Meanwhile, in a small bowl, mix the flour and 60 ml (¼ cup) of water to make a batter. Place the panko breadcrumbs on a plate. Coat the seitan in the batter and make sure it's fully coated, then toss in the breadcrumbs. Gently lower the seitan into the oil and deep-fry for 3 minutes or until golden brown. Drain on paper towel. Make a bed with the warm lentils on a large serving plate and top with the mushroom, tomato and samphire mixture, followed by the seitan. Garnish with dill fronds, or another herb of choice and serve. ▪

Malaysian vegetable-stuffed tofu with spicy peanut sauce

Serves 4
Preparation time: 40 minutes

INGREDIENTS

- 500 g (1 lb 2 oz) tofu, cut into large triangles about 1 cm (½ in) thick
- 500–750 ml (2–3 cups) organic sunflower oil, for deep-frying
- 60 ml (¼ cup) mirin
- 2 tablespoons shoyu
- 1 tablespoon brown rice vinegar
- 70 g (2½ oz) mung bean sprouts
- ½ long cucumber, deseeded, julienned
- 50 g (1¾ oz) coriander (cilantro) stalks and leaves

PEANUT SAUCE

- 130 g (½ cup) peanut butter (100% peanuts)
- 40 ml (1¼ fl oz) mirin
- 25 ml (¾ fl oz) pure maple syrup
- 2 tablespoons tomato paste (concentrated purée)
- ½ teaspoon nanami (shichimi) togarashi
- 60 ml (¼ cup) freshly squeezed lemon juice
- 2 tablespoons brown rice vinegar
- 2 tablespoons shoyu
- 1 garlic clove, grated
- 2 cm (¾ in) piece of ginger, peeled and grated

I got the idea for this dish from the wonderful cook Samantha Koch (@healthyhappy.biz) who was also a guest on the women's cooking project I ran. I invited women chefs and home cooks to present their culinary creations during a series of dinners in Amsterdam. Samantha told me that her father, who is originally from Malaysia, makes this dish regularly. When I saw it, I knew it would be good. I thought, 'This is my kind of dish' and decided to make my own version of it. It is a wonderful dish from the Malaysian cuisine, with a spicy, rich and explosive peanut butter sauce. The bite of the fried tofu, the crunch and freshness of the vegetables and the luscious sauce make it a dish to indulge in.

Tip: When you cut the tofu triangles, make sure they are large enough to fill with the vegetables.

METHOD

Gently wrap the tofu triangles in a clean tea towel and press to remove the excess liquid.

Heat the oil in a heavy-based saucepan (it should reach 4 cm/1½ in up the side of the pan) over high heat until it reaches 180°C (350°F). The oil is ready when two wooden chopsticks dipped into the oil sizzle vigorously around their edges. Deep-fry the tofu triangles for 1–2 minutes, until crisp and golden brown. Drain on paper towel.

Place the deep-fried tofu, mirin, shoyu and brown rice vinegar in a saucepan and simmer over medium heat, turning the tofu occasionally, for 3–4 minutes, until most of the liquid has evaporated.

Bring 500 ml (2 cups) of water to a gentle boil over medium–high heat. Add the mung bean sprouts and boil for 1 minute, then drain.

To make the peanut sauce, place the peanut butter, mirin, maple syrup, tomato paste, nanami togarashi, lemon juice, brown rice vinegar, shoyu, garlic, ginger and 100 ml (3½ fl oz) of water in a saucepan. Whisking constantly, bring to a gentle boil over medium heat and simmer, while continuing to whisk, for 1 minute. Remove from the heat.

Slice open each tofu triangle and stuff with a generous amount of cucumber, mung bean sprouts and coriander. Scoop the peanut sauce onto individual plates, position two stuffed tofu triangles delicately on top and serve. ▪

Grilled mushroom & seitan satay skewers

~~~~~~~~

Makes 10
Preparation time: 20 minutes

INGREDIENTS

- 500 g (1 lb 2 oz) oyster mushrooms
- 300 g (10½ oz) seitan, cut into bite-sized chunks
- 2 tablespoons olive oil
- sea salt and black pepper
- thinly sliced spring onion (scallion), to serve

This dish will satisfy all your cravings for something meaty, grilled, fatty and smoky. Make it for people who are scared that vegan food might be too boring or mild. The mushrooms and the seitan get a wonderful brown colour from the grill and the umami flavour is very dominant. Make it when you're barbecuing or just use a chargrill pan if you are making it at home.

METHOD

Alternately thread the oyster mushrooms and seitan onto 10 skewers. Preheat a barbecue grill plate on medium–high or a chargrill pan over medium–high heat. Drizzle over the olive oil, then add the skewers. Sprinkle generously with salt and black pepper and sauté the skewers for about 5 minutes each side, until very well grilled with dark brown edges. Season generously again and serve hot straight from the barbecue or pan, with a little spring onion scattered over the top. ∎

Tofu fish & broken potatoes

~~~~~~~~~

Serves 4
Preparation time: 35 minutes
Wait time: 45 minutes

INGREDIENTS

- sea salt
- 1.5 kg (3 lb 5 oz) potatoes, unpeeled
- 90 ml (3 fl oz) olive oil
- black pepper
- 6 pieces (about 100 g/3½ oz) koya dofu (freeze-dried tofu)
- 90 ml (3 fl oz) mirin
- 60 ml (¼ cup) shoyu
- 2 tablespoons brown rice vinegar
- 100 g (⅔ cup) plain unbleached (all-purpose) flour
- 100 g (3½ oz) rice flour
- 1 teaspoon ground turmeric
- 150 ml (5 fl oz) sparkling water
- 500–750 ml (2–3 cups) organic sunflower oil, for deep-frying
- 2 sheets of nori

TO SERVE

- sea salt
- nanami (shichimi) togarashi
- finely chopped red onion
- finely chopped spring onion (scallion)

This is a great party dish that you can make and eat with friends. Fish and chips is an English classic that everyone likes. This version is completely plant-based with some Japanese and Israeli tweaks. The broken/torn potatoes get so golden brown and crisp that you won't be able to stop eating them.

Dry tofu is not easy to find (see 'Special ingredients' on page 287), but once you make the effort, you'll get hooked on it just like me and it will be worth it. If you can't find dry tofu, replace it with normal tofu that you have dried in a clean kitchen towel, skipping the soaking step as it's not necessary for normal tofu.

METHOD

Preheat the oven to 180°C (350°F) fan-forced.

Pour 2 litres (8 cups) of water into a large saucepan, add 1 teaspoon of salt and bring to the boil. Add the potatoes, reduce the heat to a simmer and cook for 20–30 minutes, until soft but still al dente. Drain and set aside until cool enough to handle, then use your hands to break the potatoes into rough 2–3 cm (¾–1¼ in) chunks. Place on a baking tray, then drizzle over the olive oil and season with ½ teaspoon of salt and a generous grind of black pepper. Roast in the oven for 45 minutes or until very crisp and golden brown.

Meanwhile, place the koya dofu in a bowl. Cover with water and soak for about 3–4 minutes, until the tofu expands and hydrates. Use your hands to squeeze out 70 per cent of the water from the tofu, then cut each piece in half lengthways to form two long, thin pieces.

Place the koya dofu, mirin, shoyu, brown rice vinegar and 120 ml (4 fl oz) of water in a saucepan over medium heat and bring to a gentle boil. Cook, covered, for about 5 minutes, until most of the liquid has evaporated.

In a bowl, combine the plain flour, rice flour, turmeric and sparkling water. Whisk briefly until just combined — don't overmix.

Heat the sunflower oil in a heavy-based saucepan (it should reach 4 cm/1½ in up the side of the pan) over high heat until it reaches 180°C (350°F). The oil is ready when two wooden chopsticks dipped into the oil sizzle vigorously around their edges.

Cut the nori the same size as the koya dofu pieces, then place a piece of nori on top of each piece of koya dofu. Dredge the koya dofu in the batter, making sure each piece is completely coated, then deep-fry for about 1 minute each side, until crisp and golden brown. Drain on paper towel and sprinkle with salt and nanami togarashi.

Serve the tofu fish next to the potatoes on a serving plate, with finely chopped red onion and spring onion scattered over the top. Devour while hot. ∎

ROOT
VEGETABLES

ROOT

VEGETABLES

Root vegetables

STRENGTH &
CONFIDENCE

~~~~

Root vegetables grow underground. They connect the stem of the plant to the ground. Roots absorb water and minerals from the ground and provide them to the whole plant. Roots are a source of energy, many minerals and vitamins. Energetically speaking, root vegetables give strength and power and are grounding. Root vegetables nourish the lower abdomen, energise the legs and male sexual organs. They are an important element of the daily diet.

Root vegetables are mainly harvested, available and eaten from late summer until the end of winter, a cold period that calls for more strengthening warming foods like this. During this time in the Netherlands you can often find parsnips, parsley roots, salsify, burdock and celeriac in farmers' markets and organic food stores. It is important to consume the strengthening element in the foods all year round so I recommend eating root vegetables that are available during every season.

This is another food group that is often underestimated in a mainstream plant-based diet. I would love you to bring these somewhat old-fashioned and forgotten vegetables to the front of your kitchen counter. I hope that you will, like me, enjoy their sweetness, earthiness and roughness and explore many new, exciting ways to make them delicious, attractive and irresistible. ∎

Indian-spiced roasted salsify with cucumber guacamole

Serves 4
Preparation time: 15 minutes
Wait time: 30 minutes

INGREDIENTS

- sea salt
- 8 salsify, peeled
  (cut in half if very long)
- 60 ml (¼ cup) olive oil
- ½ teaspoon ground cumin
- ½ teaspoon ground turmeric
- ½ teaspoon curry powder
- black pepper

CUCUMBER GUACAMOLE

- 2 avocados
- 2 teaspoons freshly
  squeezed lime juice
- 1 garlic clove, grated
- 1 red onion, finely chopped
- 2 teaspoons olive oil
- 1 long cucumber,
  deseeded, grated
- 10 g (⅓ oz) coriander
  (cilantro) leaves, chopped
- 2 cm (¾ in) long red chilli,
  finely chopped
- 2 cm (¾ in) long green
  chilli, finely chopped
- ½ teaspoon sea salt
- black pepper

Salsify is an old-fashioned vegetable that is used in northern European countries. It is often called the 'asparagus of the north'. It is rich in umami flavour and reminds many people of oysters. It's one of the most delicious forgotten vegetables. Salsify is available in abundance in northern Europe, and is really worth discovering. I guarantee you that it tastes so good that you're going to fall in love with it.

I made the guacamole with cucumber so that its freshness contrasts with the earthiness of the salsify — in other words, perfection. When you peel salsify, it tends to go brown so people often put it in lemon water to keep the colour bright. I prefer to time the peeling for just before I put it in the boiling water, so it doesn't have time to oxidise. If salsify is not available, you can use any other root vegetable — carrot, turnip or parsnip — or simply replace it with white asparagus (in this case, shorten the cooking and baking time).

METHOD

Preheat the oven to 180°C (350°F) fan-forced.

Bring 1.5 litres (6 cups) of water and a pinch of salt to the boil in a large saucepan. Add the salsify and gently boil for 10–15 minutes, until just tender. Drain and transfer the salsify to a baking tray, then add the olive oil, cumin, turmeric, curry powder, ¼ teaspoon of sea salt and a generous grind of black pepper. Toss to combine, then transfer to the oven and roast for 20–30 minutes, turning halfway through cooking, until the salsify is a deep golden brown.

Meanwhile, to make the cucumber guacamole, use a fork to mash the avocado and lime juice in a bowl. Add the garlic, most of the red onion, the olive oil, cucumber, coriander, red and green chilli, sea salt and a generous grind of black pepper.

Serve the salsify on a bed of the cucumber guacamole, sprinkle over the remaining red onion and get ready to fall in love. ∎

Parsnip & cauliflower soup with crispy garlic bruschetta

Serves 4
Preparation time: 20 minutes

INGREDIENTS

- 2 tablespoons olive oil
- 2 leeks, white part only, cut into chunks
- 2 large parsnips (about 500 g/ 1 lb 2 oz), cut into chunks
- ½ head of cauliflower (about 500 g/1 lb 2 oz), cut into florets
- sea salt
- 1 garlic clove, chopped
- 1 teaspoon oregano leaves
- ground white pepper
- 1 tablespoon freshly squeezed lemon juice

GARLIC BRUSCHETTA

- 3 tablespoons olive oil
- ¼ loaf good-quality sourdough bread, sliced
- sea salt
- 1 garlic clove, cut in half

Silky, smooth and comforting. This soup is perfect for a chilly afternoon or a grey day at home. It will comfort you in your melancholy (of course, you can also make it when you're extremely happy). I use the white part of the leek to preserve the nice bright colour of the soup. Don't throw away the greens of the leek — use them in another dish or sauté them as a garnish for this soup.

METHOD

Heat the olive oil in a large saucepan over medium heat. Add the leek, parsnip, cauliflower and ¼ teaspoon of salt and sauté for 5 minutes. Add the garlic and oregano and sauté for another 1–2 minutes, adding a little water if the base of the pan starts to dry out. Add 1 litre (4 cups) of water, 1 teaspoon of salt and white pepper, to taste. Bring to the boil, then reduce the heat to low and simmer, covered, for 10–15 minutes, until the vegetables are tender.

Using a stick blender, blend the soup until smooth and creamy. Simmer for a final 1–2 minutes, then remove from the heat and add the lemon juice.

Meanwhile, to make the garlic bruschetta, heat the olive oil in a frying pan over medium heat. Add the bread and toast for 1–2 minutes each side, until crisp and golden brown. Sprinkle with salt, then rub the cut halves of the garlic on both sides of the bruschetta.

Divide the soup among bowls and serve with the garlic bruschetta on top. ▪

Roast parsnip salad with spicy coriander dressing

Serves 4
Preparation time: 20 minutes
Wait time: 30 minutes

INGREDIENTS

- 4 large parsnips (about 800 g/1 lb 12 oz), cut into 3–4 cm (1¼–1½ in) chunks
- sea salt
- 135 ml (4½ fl oz) olive oil
- 1 teaspoon ground coriander seeds
- black pepper
- 600 g (1 lb 5 oz) turnip greens, roughly chopped (or use rocket/arugula)
- 1 tablespoon mirin
- 200 g (7 oz) feto (fermented tofu), crumbled
- 100 g (3½ oz) pitted black olives, roughly chopped

CORIANDER DRESSING

- 30 g (1 oz) coriander (cilantro) leaves and stalks
- 30 g (1 oz) parsley leaves and stalks
- 90 ml (3 fl oz) olive oil
- ½ teaspoon sea salt
- 4 cm (1½ in) long green chilli, chopped
- 4 cm (1½ in) long red chilli, chopped
- 2 garlic cloves, sliced
- 60 ml (¼ cup) freshly squeezed lemon juice

Parsnips are definitely one of my favourite vegetables. I only discovered them when I moved to the Netherlands. If you prepare them in the right manner, their texture and sweet taste will be satisfying and pleasant. You'll be surprised how well all the different textures and tastes in this salad combine. What is revolutionary for me about this recipe is the discovery and renaissance of these old-fashioned vegetables. It still surprises me how wonderful they taste with a little help from some southern European and Asian friends. This salad is golden, it's green, it's rich, sour and umami. It's a dish you absolutely can't miss!

METHOD

Preheat the oven to 180°C (350°F) fan-forced.

Bring 1.5 litres (6 cups) of water to the boil in a large saucepan. Add the parsnip and a pinch of salt and boil for 5–6 minutes, until just tender but still al dente. Drain and transfer the parsnip to a baking tray and add 90 ml (3 fl oz) of the olive oil, the ground coriander, 1 teaspoon of sea salt and a generous grind of black pepper. Toss to combine, then transfer to the oven and roast for 30 minutes until the parsnip is a deep golden brown.

Meanwhile, to make the coriander dressing, place the coriander, parsley, olive oil, salt, green and red chilli, garlic and lemon juice in a blender or food processor and blend or process until well combined.

Heat the remaining 3 tablespoons of olive oil in a large saucepan over high heat. Add the turnip greens and a pinch of salt and sauté for 1 minute. Add the mirin and sauté for a few seconds, then remove from the heat and strain off any water in the pan.

In a salad bowl, add the roasted parsnip, turnip greens, feto, olives and coriander dressing and toss to combine. Serve immediately and be amazed at how fantastic this dish tastes. ∎

Light Japanese broth with fried goma dofu (sesame tofu)

Serves 4
Preparation time: 40 minutes

INGREDIENTS

- 60 g (2 oz) kuzu
- 250 ml (1 cup) cold water
- 2 tablespoons hulled (white) tahini
- 2 tablespoons mirin
- 2 tablespoons shiro miso
- 10 cm (4 in) piece of kombu
- 5 g (¼ oz) sachet of dashi powder
- 150 g (5½ oz) daikon, finely grated
- 4 cm (1½ in) piece of ginger, peeled and finely grated
- 2 tablespoons shoyu
- 500–750 ml (2–3 cups) organic sunflower oil, for deep-frying
- 60 g (2 oz) arrowroot powder
- chopped spring onion (scallion), to serve

This recipe requires quite a bit of technique, so only make it if you are comfortable working with thickening starches like arrowroot, cornstarch or kuzu, and if you're comfortable with deep-frying. This recipe involves the subtleties of traditional Japanese cuisine, although you won't find anything like this in Japan — this is my take on Japanese cuisine.

The broth is very light and the ginger makes it spicy and fresh. Goma dofu is a type of tofu made from ground sesame seeds or sesame butter (in my recipe I use tahini). The goma dofu has a special creamy and gooey texture and, after deep-frying, it almost melts in your mouth. It's this subtlety of textures, tastes and colours that makes this quiet dish so outspoken.

METHOD

Place the kuzu, cold water, tahini, mirin and miso in a saucepan and whisk to combine. Place over medium heat and bring to a gentle boil, whisking constantly. As the mixture heats, the ingredients will start to thicken. When the mixture is too thick to whisk, switch to a wooden spoon and keep stirring for 2–3 minutes, until the mixture is so thick it begins to feel like a thick glue and it's hard to stir. Don't worry — that's exactly how it should be! The mixture is ready when it turns more translucent and bubbles start to appear through the thick mass. Immediately transfer the mixture to a heatproof bowl or container and set aside to cool. Try to smooth the surface with the back of a wooden spoon, but don't worry if it's not completely level.

Combine 1 litre (4 cups) of water, the kombu and dashi powder in a saucepan and bring to a gentle simmer. Add the daikon and ginger and simmer (without boiling) over low heat for 1 minute, then add the shoyu and continue to simmer for another 1–2 minutes.

Cut the cooled goma dofu into 2 cm (¾ in) cubes — it will still be gooey but don't worry, it will still work!

~~~~~~~~~~~~~~~~

Heat the oil in a heavy-based saucepan (it should reach 4 cm/1½ in up the side of the pan) over high heat until it reaches 180°C (350°F). The oil is ready when two wooden chopsticks dipped into the oil sizzle vigorously around their edges.

Toss the goma dofu in the arrowroot to coat, then carefully lower the cubes into the hot oil and deep-fry for about 1 minute, until golden brown. Drain on paper towel.

Discard the kombu and divide the broth among bowls. Top with the goma dofu and serve this delicate dish fresh and hot as soon as it's ready, with chopped spring onion scattered over the top. ▪

Roasted celeriac with cucumber tzatziki & miso-roasted cherry tomatoes

Serves 4
Preparation time: 45 minutes

INGREDIENTS

- 1 long cucumber, deseeded, cut into matchsticks
- sea salt
- 1 celeriac, peeled and cut into 1 cm (½ in) thick rounds
- 60 ml (¼ cup) olive oil
- black pepper
- ½ teaspoon ground turmeric
- ½ teaspoon ground cumin
- ½ teaspoon curry powder
- 400 g (14 oz) silken tofu
- 1 tablespoon umesu
- 2 tablespoons freshly squeezed lemon juice
- 2 garlic cloves, 1 roughly chopped, 1 finely chopped
- 1 tablespoon white almond butter
- 350 g (12½ oz) cherry tomatoes
- 2 cm (¾ in) piece of ginger, finely chopped
- 1 tablespoon dark (red) miso paste

During the pandemic, when restaurants were closed, my clients asked me to cook for them at home — a few courses and a wine selection. Word went round and not only did my circle of clients get wider but my budget for ingredients and natural wines became unlimited. I had to come up with dishes that made people feel as if they were experiencing fine dining in a restaurant. Most of the recipes in this book come from home cooking favourites but a few are fancier — like this one.

What makes a dish impressive? Polarity! Working with opposites — textures, temperatures and tastes — in the same dish makes it exciting, explosive and impressive. The process itself doesn't have to be complex.

In this dish, the celeriac is roasted to a pleasurable golden crust and is supported by the Indian spices. Tzatziki is a fresh Greek yoghurt soup with cucumber — in this recipe I make it with silken tofu. The miso-roasted tomatoes are full of umami and spicy flavours that give a kick and contrast to the whole dish.

If guests are coming over and you want to prepare this meal in advance, you can make all the elements beforehand. Shortly before serving, warm the celeriac in the oven, finish roasting the tomatoes for 1–2 minutes and serve the tzatziki straight from the fridge.

METHOD

Preheat the oven to 180°C (350°F) fan-forced.

Place the cucumber in a small bowl with ⅛ teaspoon of salt, then mix lightly and allow to stand for 30 minutes. Squeeze the excess liquid from the cucumber and discard.

~~~~~~~~~~~~~~~~~~~~~~~~~~~~

Bring 1.5 litres (6 cups) of water and ¼ teaspoon of salt to the boil in a large saucepan. Add the celeriac and boil for about 10 minutes, until just tender but still al dente.

Drain the celeriac and transfer to a baking tray. Drizzle with 3 tablespoons of the olive oil and sprinkle ovesalt, a generous grind of black pepper, the turmeric, ground cumin and curry powder. Transfer to the oven and roast for 30–45 minutes, until the celeriac is crisp and golden brown.

Meanwhile, drain the water from the silken tofu and place it in a mixing bowl. Add the umesu, lemon juice, roughly chopped garlic clove, almond butter, ½ teaspoon of salt and a generous grind of black pepper, and mix with a stick blender until smooth. Add the drained cucumber and stir together with a spoon.

Heat the remaining 1 tablespoon of olive oil in a frying pan or wok over high heat. Add the tomatoes, ginger, finely chopped garlic clove and a pinch of salt and sauté for 1 minute. Add the dark miso paste and sauté for 30 seconds. Make sure the tomatoes soften but retain their shape (the cooking time will depend on how ripe the tomatoes are).

Divide the celeriac among plates, top with the cucumber tzatziki and roasted cherry tomatoes and serve. ∎

Beetroot, Jerusalem artichoke & caper quiche

〜〜〜〜〜

Serves 4
Preparation time: 35 minutes
Wait time: 1 hour
Equipment: 25–30 cm (10–12 in) round tart tin

INGREDIENTS

- 300 g (10½ oz) red beetroot (beets), very thinly sliced
- 300 g (10½ oz) Jerusalem artichokes, thinly sliced
- sea salt
- 100 g (⅔ cup) cashews, soaked in water for 30 minutes and up to overnight
- 600 g (1 lb 5 oz) silken tofu
- 2 shallots, sliced
- 2 garlic cloves, roughly chopped
- 2 tablespoons shiro miso
- 1 tablespoon umesu
- 2 tablespoons soy cream
- ½ teaspoon mustard
- 1 tablespoon freshly squeezed lemon juice
- black pepper
- 100 g (3½ oz) capers in brine, drained and roughly chopped

PASTRY

- 300 g (2 cups) plain unbleached (all-purpose) flour
- 75 ml (2½ fl oz) olive oil, plus extra for drizzling
- 2 tablespoons (brown) rice syrup
- 1 teaspoon sea salt
- 2 tablespoons apple cider vinegar

This quiche is full of deep earthy and umami flavours. The capers give it just the right bite and sour-spicy twist that it needs to lift it up. It's for quiche lovers, earth lovers, winter lovers and those who want to be convinced of how good tofu can taste.

METHOD

Preheat the oven to 180°C (350°F) fan-forced. Line a 25–30 cm (10–12 in) round tart tin with baking paper.

Fill two saucepans with 1 cm (½ in) of water and bring to the boil over high heat. Add the beetroot and Jerusalem artichokes to separate saucepans and season each pan with ¼ teaspoon of salt. Reduce the heat to medium and simmer, covered, for about 15 minutes, until tender, but not too soft. Drain and set aside.

Meanwhile, drain the cashews and add them to the bowl of a food processor, along with the silken tofu, shallot, garlic, shiro miso, umesu, soy cream, mustard, lemon juice and a generous grind of black pepper. Blitz until smooth, then stir through the capers.

To make the pastry, in a large bowl, place the flour, olive oil, rice syrup, salt, apple cider vinegar and 125 ml (4 fl oz) of cold water. Use a spoon to combine the ingredients, then use your hands to quickly bring the dough together without kneading. Transfer the dough to the prepared tin, then evenly press and push the dough to cover the base and side of the tin. This is a soft, rich, oily dough that is easy to mould, but if you're having trouble, refrigerate the dough for 30 minutes, to firm it up and make it easier to handle.

Spread one-quarter of the tofu mixture over the base of the pastry and add a layer of Jerusalem artichoke. Cover with another quarter of the tofu mixture, followed by a layer of beetroot. Repeat the layering process, finishing with the beetroot, then drizzle generously with olive oil and sprinkle with black pepper. Transfer the quiche to the oven and bake for 1 hour until golden brown (cover with foil if it starts to brown too quickly). The quiche can be eaten immediately, but it will taste even better the next day. Simply reheat in the oven. ∎

Salsify sautéed in spicy miso with tomato–lime salsa

~~~~~~~~~~~~

Serves 4
Preparation time: 20 minutes

INGREDIENTS

- sea salt
- 16 large salsify, peeled
  (cut in half if very long)
- 70 g (2½ oz) dark (red) miso
- 60 ml (¼ cup) mirin
- 60 ml (¼ cup) freshly
  squeezed lemon juice
- ¼ teaspoon pul biber
  (Aleppo pepper)
- 2 tablespoons (brown) rice syrup
- 2 tablespoons olive oil
- 300 g (10½ oz) cherry
  tomatoes, finely chopped
- 1 tablespoon freshly
  squeezed lime juice
- 1 shallot, diced

This dish is a wonderful and dynamic combination of earthiness, sweetness, lightness and the acidic tomato salsa gives it a stimulating, ebullient feel. I think that salsify tastes way better than asparagus and definitely deserves more of us cooking with it. I hope that, after eating this, you will be convinced too. If you can't find salsify, you can use white asparagus or even turnips.

METHOD

Bring 1 litre (4 cups) of water and ½ teaspoon of salt to the boil in a large saucepan. Add the salsify, reduce the heat to medium and cook, covered, for 15 minutes. Drain.

Meanwhile, in a small bowl add the miso, mirin, lemon juice, pul biber and rice syrup and whisk to combine.

Heat the olive oil in a saucepan over medium–high heat. Add the salsify and sauté for 3 minutes until golden brown, then add the miso dressing and sauté for another 1–2 minutes. Remove from the heat.

In a bowl, combine the tomato with ⅛ teaspoon of salt, the lime juice and shallot.

Serve the salsify and miso dressing on individual plates or a serving plate, topped with the tomato mixture. ▪

Parsnip & carrot croquettes

~~~~~~~~~~

Makes about 30
Preparation time: 20 minutes

INGREDIENTS

- 1 carrot (about 90 g/3 oz), grated
- 1 parsnip (about 120 g/4½ oz), grated
- 400 g (14 oz) silken tofu, drained
- 100 g (⅔ cup) unbleached plain (all-purpose) flour
- ½ teaspoon sea salt
- 500–750 ml (2–3 cups) organic sunflower oil, for deep-frying

This is a fun and nice party snack that you can make for your family and friends to show them how rich and indulgent plant-based food can be. You can make these croquettes with a dipping sauce of shoyu, rice syrup and lemon on the side, but honestly, I love to eat them just as they are. When it comes to these croquettes, less is more.

METHOD

In a bowl, combine the carrot, parsnip, silken tofu, flour and sea salt and mix well with a spoon.

Heat the oil in a heavy-based saucepan (it should reach 4 cm/1½ in up the side of the pan) over high heat until it reaches 180°C (350°F). The oil is ready when two wooden chopsticks dipped into the oil sizzle vigorously around their edges. Using an ice-cream scoop or a regular spoon, place small quantities of the batter into the hot oil and deep-fry for 2–3 minutes, until crisp and golden brown.

Remove the croquettes from the oil and drain on paper towel, then serve immediately. Have fun! ▪

SWEET ROUND

VEGETABLES

Sweet round vegetables

CALMING &
COMFORTING

~~~~

Sweet round vegetables are not really an official biological group.
It's a group of vegetables that is often referred to in macrobiotics
as vegetables that grow more or less at ground level. They often
have a somewhat round shape and always taste sweet. This
categorisation might be a bit unfamiliar, but in the philosophy of
my cuisine — acknowledging foods for the properties that they
bring to our bodies — I believe it makes complete sense.

Some vegetables that I include in this group are roots (turnips,
sweet potatoes), root tubers (Jerusalem artichokes), flowers
(cauliflower), leaves (cabbage), bulbs (onion, shallots, fennel),
stems (kohlrabi) and fruits (pumpkin, courgette).

These vegetables have a relaxing, soothing and comforting effect
on the body. They are related to the middle section of the upper body
and nourish the pancreas, stomach and spleen. They are all rich with
complex carbohydrates and have a mild, naturally sweet flavour.
Just like whole grains and beans, they digest slowly and provide a
steady supply of sugar to the blood, which allows the sugar level
in the blood to be more stable and even. Eating these vegetables
provides a steady, balanced calm energy over a longer period of time.
Emotionally, they give stability and balance out extreme emotions.
Most of the vegetables in this chapter are available in late summer
and the beginning of autumn. ∎

Roasted fennel with pumpkin seed tahini

~~~~~~~~

Serves 4
Preparation time: 15 minutes
Wait time: 45 minutes

INGREDIENTS

- sea salt
- 4 fennel bulbs, including green tops, cut in half lengthways into 2 cm (¾ in) thick slabs (cut larger bulbs into three)
- 3 tablespoons olive oil
- black pepper

PUMPKIN SEED TAHINI

- 100 g (3½ oz) pumpkin (pepita) seed paste
- ½ teaspoon sea salt
- 1 tablespoon freshly squeezed lemon juice
- 1 garlic clove, grated

It took me many years to fall in love with fennel. I didn't grow up with this vegetable and I ignored it over the years, because its taste was so unfamiliar. It took a bit of integration and great cooking methods (like the one in this recipe) for it to grow on me. The fennel in this recipe is smooth and elegant and full of subtle flavour. The pumpkin seed tahini is creamy and elegant — together they form a very comforting, smooth and full bite.

I use pumpkin seed paste to make the pumpkin seed tahini. You can find this paste in most organic food stores. In general, it's fun to play with pumpkin seed or sunflower seed paste (instead of sesame paste) to make tahini. I'm curious to see how you like this one.

METHOD

Preheat the oven to 180°C (350°F) fan-forced.

Bring 1.5 litres (6 cups) of water to the boil in a large saucepan over high heat. Add ¼ teaspoon of salt and the fennel and cook for about 10 minutes, until just tender but still al dente. Drain, then transfer the fennel to a baking tray. Drizzle over the olive and season with ⅛ teaspoon of salt and a generous grind of black pepper. Roast in the oven for 45 minutes until golden brown with darkened edges.

To make the pumpkin seed tahini, place all the ingredients and 75 ml (2½ fl oz) of water in a bowl and whisk to combine. It should have the consistency of mayonnaise — add a little extra water if it's too thick or a little more pumpkin seed paste if it's too thin, and whisk again.

Serve the fennel warm with the pumpkin seed tahini spooned over the top. ▪

Nimono with kohlrabi, pumpkin, shiitake & koya dofu

Serves 4
Preparation time: 20 minutes
Wait time: 45 minutes

INGREDIENTS

- 10 cm (4 in) piece of kombu
- 10 dried shiitake mushrooms
- 10 g (¼ oz) sachet of dashi powder
- 1 large kohlrabi (or 2 small), peeled and cut into large chunks
- 750 g (1 lb 11 oz) orange or green Hokkaido pumpkin, cut into large chunks
- 4 pieces (about 65 g/2¼ oz) koya dofu (freeze-dried tofu)
- 500–750 ml (2–3 cups) organic sunflower oil, for deep-frying
- 60 ml (¼ cup) mirin
- 2 tablespoons shoyu
- ½ teaspoon yuzu (or lemon juice)

Nimono is a general name for a simple Japanese home-style stew — a steaming, umami broth full of all kinds of tasty things like vegetables, meat or tofu. The nimono in this recipe is gentle, elegant and full of deep, yet subtle flavours. Kohlrabi is definitely one of the most underestimated vegetables that we should all start to use. In this dish, it rises to its full capacity, glory and potential of flavour. When I eat it, I enjoy and memorise every little bite I take of it and count the seconds, minutes, days and weeks until I can take the next one.

You can find koya dofu in the stores mentioned in 'Shops & online stores' on page 291. Otherwise, smoked tofu will also work just fine in this recipe, with or without deep-frying.

METHOD

Place the kombu, shiitake mushrooms, dashi powder and 750 ml (3 cups) of water in a large saucepan and bring to a gentle boil. Gently place the kohlrabi and pumpkin on top of the mushrooms, then reduce the heat to a simmer and cook, covered and without stirring, for 30 minutes.

Meanwhile, soak the koya dofu in about 750 ml (3 cups) of water for about 5 minutes, until soft. Use your hands to squeeze 75 per cent of the liquid from the koya dofu, leaving just a little moisture, then thinly slice.

Heat the oil in a heavy-based saucepan (it should reach 4 cm/1½ in up the side of the pan) over high heat until it reaches 180°C (350°F). The oil is ready when two wooden chopsticks dipped into the oil sizzle vigorously around their edges. Deep-fry the koya dofu for about 1 minute, then drain on paper towel.

Using chopsticks, carefully remove the shiitake mushrooms from the broth without stirring the mixture. Cut away the mushrooms stalks and discard, and cut the mushroom caps into 5 mm (¼ in) thick slices. Place the sliced mushroom on top of the kohlrabi and pumpkin, along with the deep-fried koya dofu, and simmer for 10–15 minutes, until the vegetables are tender.

Add the mirin, shoyu and yuzu and simmer for a final 5 minutes. Divide the vegetables among deep round bowls and generously pour the broth over the top. Serve and enjoy every soft bite. ▪

A salad of red cabbage, apple & toasted chilli peanuts

~~~~~~~~~~~~~

Serves 4
Preparation time: 15 minutes

INGREDIENTS

- ½ teaspoon sea salt
- 700 g (1 lb 9 oz) red cabbage, very thinly sliced
- 1 tablespoon roasted sesame oil
- 75 g (2¾ oz) natural unsalted peanuts
- ¼ teaspoon nanami (shichimi) togarashi
- 1 tablespoon pure maple syrup
- 1 teaspoon shoyu
- 2 apples, unpeeled, cored and thinly sliced
- 100 g (3½ oz) dried cranberries

DRESSING

- 2 tablespoons apple juice concentrate
- 3 tablespoons brown rice vinegar
- 2 tablespoons umesu
- 60 ml (¼ cup) freshly squeezed lemon juice

I made this salad when I worked as a chef in the legendary lunchroom Deshima in Amsterdam. Way too early in the morning (in my terms, practically night!) I would go to their vegetable shop just beneath the restaurant to pick up my vegetables for the day. The red cabbages that had already been waiting for someone to pick them up for a few weeks were begging me to use them, and so was the shop owner. And I thought, 'Here is a great challenge'.

Let's admit it: red cabbage is not the easiest vegetable and not something I would normally jump to use with ease. This is mainly because of its rough bite and bitter flavour, which I tried to remove in this recipe by pressing it thoroughly, so there is a good chance you will finally like it. I use plenty of lemon, cranberries and sweetness to give it a very attractive sour-sweet taste. (Make sure the salad tastes really sour.) I also press the cabbage by massaging it and putting it under pressure and that gives it a more pleasant texture and less of the unpleasant taste. You can make a lot for a few days, because the more it marinates in its juices, the tastier it will become. This made it a very helpful recipe when I worked in Deshima and the wonderful magenta colour made every dish I served look like a little artwork.

METHOD

Sprinkle the salt over the cabbage, then, using your hands, massage and squeeze the cabbage for 5–10 minutes, until tender and the juice has leached out. Optional: continue to press the cabbage by placing it in a salad press or under a heavy weight for 15–30 minutes and up to overnight. This helps to remove the bitterness of the cabbage and makes it more digestible. You can skip this step but it does result in a tastier salad. Discard all the juice and place the cabbage in a salad bowl.

Heat the sesame oil in a saucepan over medium heat. Add the peanuts and toast for 2–3 minutes, until golden brown (if the peanuts are already roasted, reduce the cooking time to 1–2 minutes). Add the nanami togarashi, maple syrup and shoyu and cook for a further 2 minutes, until most of the liquid has evaporated.

To make the dressing, combine the apple juice concentrate, brown rice vinegar, umesu and lemon juice in a bowl.

Add the apple, cranberries, chilli peanuts and dressing to the cabbage and toss well to combine. Serve. ▪

Roasted swede with tomato salsa & herb chutney

Serves 4
Preparation time: 20 minutes
Cook time: 30 minutes

INGREDIENTS

- 1 swede (rutabaga), peeled and cut into 3 mm (⅛ in) thick slices
- sea salt
- 60 ml (¼ cup) olive oil
- black pepper

TOMATO SALSA

- 400 g (14 oz) tomatoes (any variety), cut into small chunks
- 1 garlic clove, grated or finely chopped
- 3 cm (1¼ in) long red chilli, finely chopped
- 3 cm (1¼ in) long green chilli, finely chopped
- ¼ teaspoon freshly squeezed lemon juice
- 2 tablespoons olive oil
- ¼ teaspoon sea salt
- black pepper

Rutabaga is an old-fashioned, forgotten vegetable. In this recipe, I bring it back to life and show you how colourful and flavourful it can be. A fun tomato salsa and a herb chutney bring Italian flavours that lift up this earthy-tasting vegetable, and bright yellows, reds and greens colours to liven up your plate. It's not always easy to bring out the tasty flavour of rutabaga, which is why many people don't like it, but this recipe enhances its natural sweetness. When we tested this recipe for the cookbook, we ended up eating the whole tray between two of us.

METHOD

Preheat the oven to 180°C (350°F) fan-forced.

Bring 1.5 litres (6 cups) of water to the boil in a large saucepan. Add the swede and a pinch of salt, then reduce the heat to a simmer and cook for 10 minutes until just tender but still al dente. Drain and transfer the swede to a baking tray in a single layer (it's okay if the edges are overlapping slightly). Drizzle with the olive oil and season with ½ teaspoon of salt and a generous grind of black pepper. Roast in the oven for 20–30 minutes, until the edges of the swede are golden brown, almost like cooked lasagne sheets.

Meanwhile, to make the tomato salsa, in a mortar, combine the tomato, garlic, red and green chilli, lemon juice, olive oil, salt and a generous grind of black pepper. Use the pestle to squash everything together — the tomatoes will release a lot of liquid, which can be spooned over the final dish. If you don't have a pestle and mortar, simply place the ingredients in a bowl and mash them using a potato masher or even the bottom of a bottle.

HERB CHUTNEY

- 25 g (1 oz) basil
  leaves and stalks
- 25 g (1 oz) parsley
  leaves and stalks
- 15 g (½ oz) coriander
  (cilantro) leaves
  and stalks
- 1 large garlic clove,
  roughly sliced
- 3 cm (1¼ in) long red
  chilli, roughly chopped
- 3 cm (1¼ in) long green
  chilli, roughly chopped
- 3 tablespoons olive oil
- 1 teaspoon freshly
  squeezed lemon juice
- ¼ teaspoon sea salt
- black pepper

To make the herb chutney, combine the basil, parsley, coriander, garlic, red and green chilli, olive oil, lemon juice, sea salt and a generous grind of black pepper in a bowl and use a stick blender to blend the ingredients to a pesto-like consistency.

To serve, place the roasted swede on a serving plate and top with the salsa and herb chutney to create beautiful contrasting colours. ∎

Roasted sunset-coloured vegetables with seitan

Serves 4
Preparation time: 15 minutes
Wait time: 45 minutes

INGREDIENTS

- 3 onions, cut into large wedges
- 1 sweet potato, cut into 3–4 cm (1¼–1½ in) wedges
- 1 large carrot, cut into 3–4 cm (1¼–1½ in) wedges
- 300 g (10½ oz) potatoes, cut into 3–4 cm (1¼–1½ in) wedges
- 2 sweet-pointed capsicums (peppers), cut into rough chunks
- 400 g (14 oz) cherry tomatoes
- 300 g (10½ oz) oyster mushrooms
- 200 g (7 oz) seitan, cut into chunks
- 135 ml (4½ fl oz) olive oil
- 1 tablespoon sea salt
- black pepper
- 1½ teaspoons sweet paprika
- 1½ teaspoons smoked paprika
- 10 garlic cloves, unpeeled

This is a wonderful dish when you don't have time to cook but you do want to eat something earthy, filling and comforting. This dish is full of deep umami and sweet flavours. It will go well with the polenta from the recipe on page 38 and a fresh salad, like the Pear, basil and roasted almond salad on page 192. I love the colours of late summer and autumn on the plate. This sunset is sensual, flavourful, warm and easy. Why not make it tonight?

METHOD

Preheat the oven to 180°C (350°F) fan-forced.

Place the onion, sweet potato, carrot, potato, capsicum, cherry tomatoes, oyster mushrooms, seitan, olive oil, salt, a generous grind of black pepper, sweet paprika, smoked paprika and unpeeled garlic cloves in a large roasting tin. Toss the ingredients together, then transfer to the oven and roast for about 45 minutes, until the vegetables are golden brown. Serve the vegetables with cooked polenta or a salad, and enjoy the sunset on your plate. ∎

Orange & fennel salad

~~~~~~~~~~

Serves 4
Preparation time: 10 minutes

INGREDIENTS

- 2 tablespoons olive oil
- 2 fennel bulbs, cut into chunks
- pinch of sea salt
- ½ teaspoon pul biber (Aleppo pepper)
- 60 ml (¼ cup) mirin
- few drops of yuzu juice
- 6 oranges, peeled and cut into large chunks
- 2 tablespoons umesu
- 2 tablespoons apple cider vinegar
- few drops of food-grade orange oil (optional)

This is a quick, summery, refreshing side dish. I love the crunchy bite of this salad. And it is even better the next day, when the fennel has had time to soften and absorb the sweet, salty dressing.

METHOD

Heat the olive oil in a frying pan over medium heat. Add the fennel and salt and sauté for 2 minutes, then add the pul biber, mirin and a few drops of yuzu juice and sauté for 1 minute.

In a salad bowl, combine the sautéed fennel, orange, umesu and apple cider vinegar. Add a few drops of orange oil (if using) to complete the aroma, and toss to combine. ∎

Broccoli, cauliflower & mushroom tempura

Serves 4
Preparation time: 15 minutes

INGREDIENTS

- 500–750 ml (2–3 cups) organic sunflower oil, for deep-frying
- 150 g (1 cup) plain unbleached (all-purpose) flour
- ½ teaspoon ground turmeric
- ½ teaspoon curry powder
- ½ teaspoon ground cumin
- 1 teaspoon yellow mustard seeds
- 265 ml (9 fl oz) sparkling water (preferably chilled)
- 250 g (9 oz) button mushrooms
- ½ head of broccoli (about 200 g/7 oz), cut into florets
- ½ head of cauliflower (about 400 g/14 oz), cut into small florets

TO SERVE

- sea salt
- ground sumac

Here is a great party or dinner snack, or for times when you crave a good bite of tempura. I love the colours and the smell of this recipe. Tempura is a great way to introduce vegetables to those who are less fond of them. Many people are reluctant to deep-fry, but this is just another cooking style that has been used traditionally in many cultures and delivers a very satisfying and appetising experience. The use of a hot flame with very hot oil can be very energising if you have an active lifestyle. I say: don't be shy; deep-fry!

METHOD

Heat the oil in a heavy-based saucepan (it should reach 4 cm/1½ in up the side of the pan) over high heat until it reaches 180°C (350°F). The oil is ready when two wooden chopsticks dipped into the oil sizzle vigorously around their edges.

Combine the flour, turmeric, curry powder, cumin and mustard seeds in a bowl. Add the sparkling water and gently stir with a whisk — do not overmix. Working in batches, dredge the vegetables in the batter to completely coat, then deep-fry for 3–4 minutes, until crisp and golden brown. Drain on paper towel and sprinkle with a generous amount of salt and sumac.

Serve hot to the great applause of your guests. ▪

Flame-roasted whole eggplant with tahini

Serves 4
Preparation time: 15 minutes
Wait time: 45 minutes

INGREDIENTS

- 4 eggplants (aubergines)
- 100 g (3½ oz) hulled (white) tahini
- 1 tablespoon freshly squeezed lemon juice
- sea salt

TO SERVE

- sea salt
- black pepper
- finely chopped red onion
- 1 garlic clove, finely chopped
- chopped parsley
- olive oil
- freshly squeezed lemon juice

It's incredible how tasty eggplant is when it is burnt on an open flame. You can easily do this on a gas cooker at home, or you can use an open fire outside. Don't be scared to take the time and allow the skin of the eggplant to burn properly on all sides. This will make the inside very soft and the flavour very smoky. This dish is one of the highlights of Israel contemporary cuisine, where whole vegetables are used and extreme cooking styles are applied to enhance their flavours to their full capacity. Your house will smell wonderfully of smoky eggplant, so open the doors, open your hearts, invite guests in and enjoy this explosive dish with them.

You can serve this as a starter or as a side on a big, shared dining table with a slice of sourdough bread, flatbread or pita bread. This dish is soft, creamy and melts in your mouth.

METHOD

Place the eggplants over a medium stovetop flame and roast for 40–45 minutes, until the skins are burned and the insides are soft (see photo on page 16).

Carefully scrape the burnt skin off the eggplants, trying to leave the flesh intact (see photo on page 172). If the skin is really burnt, this should be easy. Alternatively, slice the eggplant in half lengthways and (using a tablespoon) prise the flesh away from the skin (see photo on page 172). It's not the end of the world if the eggplant falls apart, and don't worry if some of the skin remains attached to the flesh, as it will add a lovely smoky accent to the dish.

Mix the tahini with the lemon juice and ¼ teaspoon of salt in a small bowl, then slowly drizzle in about 100 ml (3½ fl oz) of water, whisking constantly, until you achieve a yoghurt consistency.

Place the eggplant on a serving plate and drizzle the tahini sauce over the top. Sprinkle generously with sea salt, black pepper, red onion, garlic and parsley, drizzle with olive oil and lemon juice. ∎

Zucchini
baba ghanoush

Serves 4
Preparation time: 10 minutes
Wait time: 40 minutes

INGREDIENTS

- 2 zucchini (courgettes)
- 50 g (1¾ oz) hulled (white) tahini
- ¼ teaspoon sea salt
- 1 tablespoon freshly
  squeezed lemon juice
- 1 garlic clove, grated
- black pepper

TO SERVE

- chopped parsley
- olive oil
- smoked paprika (optional)
- flatbread or good-quality
  sourdough bread

You'll be surprised how pleasant this less-familiar variation on the traditional Middle Eastern dish tastes. It is very creamy and makes a great addition to a shared dining table next to delicious bread and other tapas-like foods.

METHOD

Preheat the oven to 200°C (400°F) fan-forced.

Place the whole zucchinis on a baking tray, then transfer to the oven and roast for 30–40 minutes, until the zucchini are completely soft and brown-black in colour.

Transfer the zucchini to a bowl and mash with a potato masher — they will release a lot of juice but this will help loosen the tahini. Add the tahini, salt, lemon juice, garlic and a generous grind of black pepper and mix well with a fork. Scatter chopped parsley over the top, drizzle with olive oil and sprinkle with a little smoked paprika, if you like. Serve with flatbread or good-quality sourdough bread. ∎

Caramelised sweet potatoes with thyme

~~~~~~~~~~

Serves 4
Preparation time: 5 minutes
Cook time: 1 hour

INGREDIENTS

- 60 ml (¼ cup) olive oil
- 1 teaspoon sea salt
- black pepper
- 4 sweet potatoes, unpeeled, halved lengthways
- 8 sprigs of thyme

Sweet potato is my favourite vegetable — I could eat it every day! I thought I already knew all the best recipes you can make with sweet potatoes until I learned this one from who else but Keren Rubenstein, the creator of the broad bean salad on page 81.

I met Keren when I was organising a women's cooking project where I invited women chefs to present their cooking talents. I realised that most of the good cooking I have learned was from women, starting with my mother and, more recently, my macrobiotic teachers, Valentina and Wieke Nelissen. Unfortunately, women are less known in the food scene and most of the attention goes to male chefs and writers. I wanted to create a platform where the public could meet these incredible cooks and taste their creations. Keren was one of these cooks and when we were eating her food, we cried — it was so good!

In this recipe, we lie the halved sweet potatoes cut-side down on the oven tray so the sugars drip and caramelise at the bottom of the tray. This makes the sweet potatoes very crisp. The contrast between the soft tender flesh and the crispy and very caramelised bottom is really hard to resist. The sweet potatoes will also look beautiful on your plate. Needless to say, it's so easy to make yet so impressive!

METHOD

Preheat the oven to 180°C (350°F) fan-forced.

Drizzle the olive oil over a baking tray and sprinkle with the salt and a generous grind of black pepper. Lay the sweet potato halves, cut-side down, on the tray and place a sprig of thyme under each half. Transfer to the oven and roast the sweet potato for 1 hour, checking regularly to ensure the 'caramel' released from the potato isn't burning. It's a fine balance — you want to make sure the sweet potato is crisp and golden brown, with a caramelised base, without it blackening. Don't rush this step, and wait for this magic moment. It will be worth it.

You could serve the sweet potato with the red cabbage and apple salad on page 157 but, to be honest, this dish is already amazing on its own. Try it, you won't regret it! ▪

Nishime of kohlrabi & Jerusalem artichokes with almond gravy

Serves 4
Preparation time: 10 minutes
Cook time: 25 minutes

INGREDIENTS

- pinch of sea salt
- 500 g (1 lb 2 oz) Jerusalem artichokes, halved lengthways
- 2 kohlrabi, peeled and cut into large wedges
- 80 g (⅓ cup) white almond butter
- 2 tablespoons umesu

This is simply a wonderful way to cook these vegetables and enjoy their soft, earthy and gentle flavours. You'll be surprised how creamy and tender this dish is.

METHOD

Pour 2 cm (¾ in) of water into a saucepan and bring to a simmer over medium heat. Add the salt, Jerusalem artichoke and kohlrabi, then cover and simmer for about 25 minutes, until tender. Keep an eye on the water level while the vegetables cook and top up with just under 5 mm (¼ in) more water if necessary.

Add the almond butter and umesu and mix very gently with a wooden spoon. Continue to simmer, uncovered, until most of the liquid has evaporated and you have a creamy, thick gravy.

Serve with a protein-rich dish, such as the mushroom and seitan satay on page 114 or the black bean stew with seitan on page 84. ▪

Roasted fennel on a bed of apple & kohlrabi purée

~~~~~~

Serves 4
Preparation time: 20 minutes

INGREDIENTS

- sea salt
- 1 kohlrabi, peeled and cut into large chunks
- 1 apple, peeled, cored and cut into large chunks
- 2 tablespoons olive oil
- ½ teaspoon fennel seeds
- 1 fennel bulb, stalk and bulb cut into large chunks
- 25 g (1 oz) almonds, thinly sliced
- 35 g (1¾ cups) parsley, soft stalks and leaves finely chopped
- 20 g (⅔ cup) coriander (cilantro), soft stalks and leaves finely chopped
- 4 cm (1½ in) long red chilli, finely chopped
- zest of 1 lemon

I love getting creative with local and seasonal vegetables, as in this recipe. The tastes and textures here are a little bit adventurous and promise a subtle and light experience for kohlrabi and fennel lovers. I recommend using sour apples if they are available, but any apple will do.

METHOD

Pour 1 cm (½ in) of water into a saucepan with a pinch of salt and bring to the boil over high heat. Add the kohlrabi and apple, then cover, reduce the heat to medium and simmer for about 20 minutes or until very tender. Strain the water into a heatproof bowl.

Using a stick blender, blend the kohlrabi and apple, adding enough of the cooking water to achieve a soft purée.

Heat the olive oil and fennel seeds in a frying pan over medium–high heat. Add the fennel and almonds and sauté for 3–5 minutes, until the fennel starts to brown at the edges. Add the parsley, coriander, chilli, ¼ teaspoon of salt and the lemon zest and sauté for another minute.

Spread the apple and kohlrabi purée on a serving plate and place the roasted fennel mixture delicately on top, then serve. ∎

Indian summer vegetables with tahini

~~~~~~~~~~

Serves 4
Preparation time: 15 minutes
Cook time: 30 minutes

INGREDIENTS

- 250 g (9 oz) millet
- sea salt
- 1 yellow beetroot (beet), peeled and cut into wedges
- 1 sweet potato, peeled and cut into wedges
- 200 g (7 oz) podded green peas
- ½ pointed (sweetheart) cabbage, (about 300 g/10½ oz), cut into large chunks
- 10 radishes
- 500 g (1 lb 2 oz) cherry tomatoes
- 150 g (5½ oz) hulled or unhulled (white or brown) tahini
- 2 tablespoons umesu

When the pandemic started, I wanted to nourish my body and give my immune system a good boost. I went to a farmers' market regularly and bought plenty of vegetables to make this dish almost daily. Seasonal organic produce tastes so good when prepared in a modest and daily manner like this. This simple and nourishing meal will give you a soothing, stable, calm energy and also keep you in balance. It is a great way to get a lot of vitamins, minerals and good quality carbohydrates and fibre into your body, but also to keep your body, mind and immune system in good balance.

I make a tahini sauce in this recipe, which you can vary by using pumpkin seed butter or sunflower seed butter instead of the sesame seed butter. They will all make a wonderful rich sauce next to the vegetables.

Pay attention to the cooking time of the vegetables. You need to start with the vegetables that need a longer cooking time and then continue with the ones that need a shorter cooking time. The lower part of the pan holds the vegetables that need a longer cooking time, and they will cook in the water. The upper part of the pan holds the softer vegetables that need a shorter cooking time, and they will steam. Cook the vegetables until tender, but don't overcook them.

~~~~~~~~~~~~~~~~~~~~~~~~~~~~~

METHOD

Place the millet in a pressure cooker and cover with water. Lightly swirl to wash the millet, then drain and repeat the process until the water runs clear. Return the millet to the pressure cooker and add 550 ml (18½ fl oz) of water and a pinch of salt. Bring to medium pressure and pressure cook for 15 minutes. Allow the pressure to release naturally, then open the cooker and stir the millet with a wooden spoon. Alternatively, cook the millet in a saucepan of simmering water for 30 minutes.

Pour 2–3 cm (¾–1¼ in) of water into a saucepan, add two pinches of salt and bring to a gentle boil. Add the yellow beetroot first, then the sweet potato and simmer, covered, for 10 minutes. Add the peas, pointed cabbage and radishes and simmer for another 10 minutes. Add the tomatoes and simmer for a final 10 minutes.

Meanwhile, in a bowl whisk together the tahini, umesu and 125 ml (4 fl oz) of water.

Spoon the millet onto a serving plate and arrange the vegetables in individual portions next to each other to form a colourful palette. Drizzle with the tahini sauce or pour into serving bowls and serve on the side for guests to dip the vegetables in one by one. This is as zen as you will get while using this book. ∎

GREEN VEGETABLES

GREEN

VEGETABLES

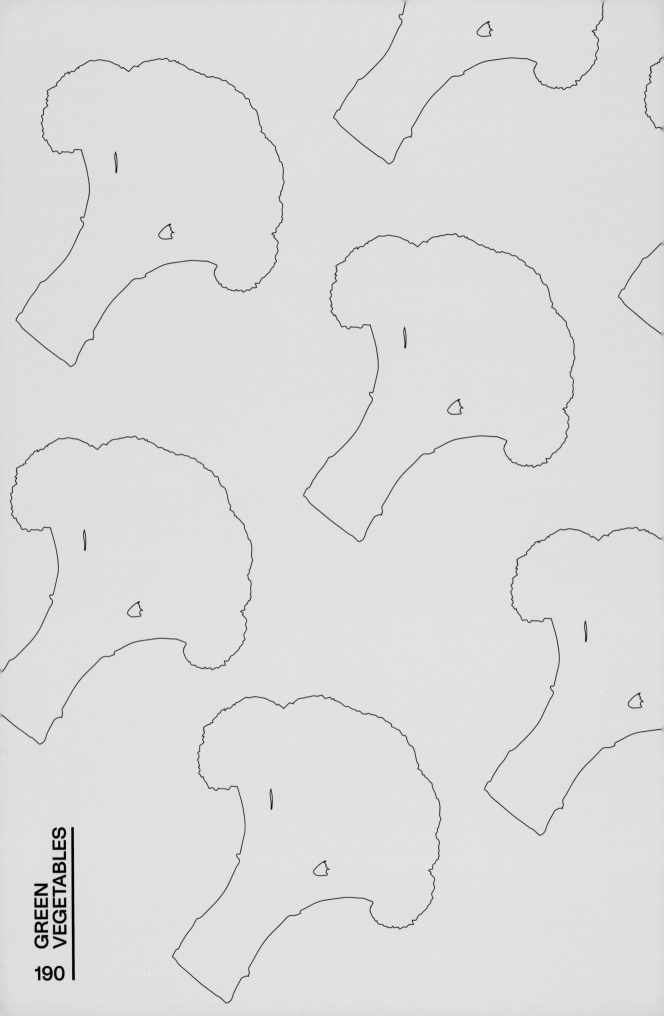

Green vegetables

**LIGHT & CALCIUM &
IRON & VITAMIN C**

~~~

The vegetables that fall into this category are usually from the leafy part of the plant. Leafy green vegetables are rich in calcium and iron and often vitamin C, which helps our bodies absorb the iron.

Green vegetables grow upwards so they provide upward energy. They uplift, open up, lighten and give upbeat oomph. Green vegetables help you express yourself better, express emotions, use your voice, get inspired, move, get ideas and in general feel lighter. Green vegetables are also very rich in fibre, which supports good digestion and strong intestines. They are a crucial part of every meal and definitely can't be skipped. ∎

Pear, basil & roasted almond salad

~~~~~~~~~

Serves 4
Preparation time: 15 minutes

INGREDIENTS

- 1 tablespoon olive oil
- 80 g (½ cup) almonds, chopped roughly
- sea salt
- 3 pears, unpeeled, cored and thinly sliced
- 80 g (2¾ oz) basil, leaves picked

SWEET AND SOUR DRESSING

- 2 tablespoons balsamic vinegar
- 1 tablespoon shoyu
- 2 tablespoons umesu
- 1½ teaspoons pure maple syrup
- 2 tablespoons freshly squeezed lemon juice

This is a perfect salad if you feel like eating something simple, fresh and light. When the hot sun is shining straight into your face, this refreshing bite is exactly what you'll crave.

METHOD

Heat the olive oil in a saucepan over medium heat. Add the almonds and 2 pinches of salt and roast, stirring constantly, for about 3 minutes, until golden brown, making sure the almonds don't burn. Immediately transfer to a bowl, to avoid further roasting or burning.

To make the dressing, combine the balsamic vinegar, shoyu, umesu, maple syrup and lemon juice in a bowl.

In a salad bowl, combine the pear, roasted almonds, basil and dressing. Serve and enjoy! ∎

A light miso soup
with plenty of greens

～～～～～

Serves 4
Preparation time: 15 minutes

INGREDIENTS

- 75 ml (2½ fl oz)
  roasted sesame oil
- 1 onion, thinly sliced
  into half moons
- 1 garlic clove, grated
- 2 cm (¾ in) piece of ginger,
  peeled and finely grated
- 1 x 10 g (¼ oz) sachet
  of dashi powder
- 2 tablespoons shiro miso
- 2 tablespoons dark (red) miso
- ½ head of broccoli (about
  250 g/9 oz), cut into florets
- 10 thin spring onions (scallions),
  cut into thirds, white and
  green parts separated
- ⅓ head of wombok
  (napa/Chinese cabbage)
  (about 350 g/12½ oz),
  cut into big chunks
- ⅛ teaspoon sea salt
- 3 tablespoons mirin
- ¼ teaspoon nanami
  (shichimi) togarashi
- 1 tablespoon shoyu

TO SERVE

- 4 cm (1½ in) piece of ginger,
  peeled and finely grated
- a few lemon slices

Miso soup is one of my signature dishes. A client who often asked me to cook for him, his friends and his family, told me that he would only invite me if I made my miso soup for him. Over the years, I have probably made thousands of miso soups. To this day it is probably one of the dishes I love to eat the most.

Miso is a paste made from soybean, salt and koji rice (Japanese mould-fermented rice). The moulded rice ferments the beans and brings out the umami flavours. Umami is the fifth taste (next to sweet, sour, bitter and salty). Most Western people are not aware of umami, but it is very important in Japanese cuisine. You can find umami in tomatoes, meat and parmesan cheese. Miso is also full of umami.

The quality of the miso you use will strongly determine how good your miso soup is. If you're into quirky fermentation (and delicious food), I recommend making your own miso paste. I promise that nothing in the world will taste as good. It's not that difficult, but the fermentation time is 8 months. For everyone else, go to 'Shops & online stores' on page 291 to find out where to buy really good miso.

This is a spring-like, summer-like, uplifting miso soup. You can, however, make it any time of the year and any time of the day, as a daily meal or for a festive meal for your friends. Miso soup is a classic. It's something that everyone always likes to eat and it makes everyone feel good. Wherever you are, whenever you are, eat a miso soup.

Note: If the spring onion is thick, use half the quantity and cut each spring onion in half lengthways.

METHOD

Heat 3 tablespoons of the sesame oil in a saucepan over medium heat. Add the onion, garlic and ginger and sauté, stirring, for 2–3 minutes, until the onion is soft and slightly golden. Add a tablespoon of water if the base of the pan starts to dry out. Add 1 litre (4 cups) of water and the dashi and bring to a simmer, without boiling. Reduce the heat to low and cook, covered, for 10 minutes.

There are two ways to add the miso to the soup. My preferred method is to dilute the misos into the soup through a sieve (see image). To do this, place the miso in a fine-mesh sieve, then lower it into the soup. Using a teaspoon, stir the miso inside the sieve until it slowly melts into the soup. Alternatively, spoon some of the soup into a heatproof bowl and whisk in the miso, then return the mixture to the soup. Continue to cook over low heat, without boiling — the low temperature will activate the enzymes in the miso without killing them — for another 1–2 minutes, until 'clouds' start to appear. At this point, remove the pan from the heat.

Heat the remaining 2 tablespoons of sesame oil in a frying pan over high heat. Add the broccoli and white part of the spring onion and sauté, stirring, for 3–4 minutes, until the broccoli starts to brown at the edges. Add the wombok, salt and the green part of the spring onion and sauté for 2–3 minutes, until starting to soften, adding a tablespoon of water if the base of the pan starts to dry out. Add the mirin, nanami togarashi and shoyu and sauté for another 1–2 minutes.

Divide the miso soup and sautéed greens among bowls, top with a little grated ginger and a slice of lemon and serve. ∎

Stir-fried pointed cabbage & apple

~~~~~~~~~~~~~~~~~~~~~~

Serves 4
Preparation time: 10 minutes

INGREDIENTS

- 1 tablespoon neutral sesame oil
- ½ head of pointed (sweetheart) cabbage, cut into big chunks
- 1 apple, unpeeled, cored and thinly sliced
- pinch of sea salt
- 2 tablespoons mirin
- 2 tablespoons freshly squeezed lemon juice
- ¼ teaspoon nanami (shichimi) togarashi

This is a quick and light sauté of pointed cabbage and apple. Green vegetables, sour tastes and sweet tastes, like the ones in this dish, are great in the morning because they are light and have a rising energy, which is the energy of the morning. Green vegetables stimulate the liver — the organ that is most active in the morning. You can also use this as a side dish next to a heavier dish, or eat it when you feel like you need a light refreshment.

METHOD

Heat the sesame oil in a frying pan or wok over medium–high heat. Add the cabbage, apple and salt and sauté, stirring, for about 2 minutes, until the cabbage is just tender, but still al dente. Add the mirin, lemon juice and nanami togarashi and sauté for another minute. Eat hot and fresh from the pan or wok. ▪

An abundance of greens with roasted hazelnuts & tomato tahini

Serves 4
Preparation time: 25 minutes

INGREDIENTS

- 90 ml (3 fl oz) olive oil
- 300 g (10½ oz) silverbeet (Swiss chard), roughly chopped
- 3 garlic cloves, 2 thinly sliced, 1 roughly chopped
- sea salt and black pepper
- 8 thin green asparagus spears, woody ends peeled, thick stalks cut in half lengthways
- 200 g (7 oz) broccolini, thick stalks cut in half lengthways
- 50 g (½ cup) skinned hazelnuts, roughly chopped
- 150 g (5½ oz) hulled (white) tahini
- 250 g (9 oz) tomatoes
- 1 tablespoon freshly squeezed lemon juice

This dish is definitely inspired by the cuisine of Tel Aviv. It is green, red, crisp, creamy, fatty, explosive, exciting and marvellous. I invented it for this cookbook, fell in love with it and immediately started to make it for my private dining clients. You can make it all year round with greens that are fresh and available in season. Use a high-intensity flame and let it lift up the whole energy of the dish. Greens are exciting, my friends, and intensity is the name of the game here.

Note: If the stems of the broccolini or asparagus are very thick, cut them lengthways.

METHOD

Heat 2 tablespoons of the olive oil in a large frying pan over high heat. Add the silverbeet, sliced garlic and a generous sprinkle of salt and pepper, then sauté for 2 minutes until the silverbeet is just tender. Remove from the pan and set aside.

Heat 2 tablespoons of the remaining olive oil in the same pan over high heat. Add the asparagus and broccolini to different parts of the pan (if there's not enough space, cook the vegetables in batches separately). Don't mix them while cooking so you can control the cooking time of each vegetable. Sprinkle with a generous amount of salt and pepper and sauté for 2–3 minutes, until lightly golden but still crisp, adding 2 tablespoons of water if the base of the pan starts to dry out. Remove the vegetables from the pan and set aside.

In the same pan, heat the final 2 tablespoons of olive oil over medium heat. Add the hazelnuts and cook, stirring constantly, for 1–2 minutes, until golden brown. Immediately remove from the pan and set aside.

In the bowl of a food processor, place the tahini, tomatoes, ¼ teaspoon of salt, the lemon juice and roughly chopped garlic, and blitz to form a thin dressing. Spread the tomato tahini in a circle on serving plates and top with the greens. Finish with the hazelnuts, then serve and enjoy. ∎

Sautéed oyster mushrooms, Chinese cabbage, spring onion & broccolini

Serves 4
Preparation time: 15 minutes

INGREDIENTS

- 3 tablespoons roasted sesame oil
- 2 garlic cloves, finely chopped
- 4 cm (1½ in) piece of ginger, finely chopped
- ¼ teaspoon chilli flakes
- 150 g (5½ oz) oyster mushrooms, thinly sliced
- ½ wombok (napa/ Chinese cabbage), cut into large chunks
- 4 spring onions (scallions), cut in half lengthways and then in half crossways
- 200 g (7 oz) broccolini, thick stalks cut in half lengthways
- 60 ml (¼ cup) mirin
- 2 tablespoons shoyu

This is a really tasty dish full of greens, which will give you strong uplifting energy and get you on the move. It's light, fresh, super tasty and comes together in a flash. The delicious combination of Asian-style sweet, umami, spicy flavours makes it hard to stop eating.

METHOD

Heat the sesame oil in a frying pan or wok over high heat. Add the garlic, ginger and chilli flakes and sauté for a few seconds, then add the mushrooms, wombok, spring onion and broccolini. Sauté for 2–3 minutes, until the vegetables are just tender. Add the mirin and shoyu and sauté for a few more seconds.

Serve hot and fresh straight from the pan or wok. ∎

Fattoush

〜〜〜〜〜

Serves 4
Preparation time: 15 minutes

INGREDIENTS

- 500–750 ml (2–3 cups) organic sunflower oil, for deep-frying
- 2 mini white or wholemeal (whole wheat) pita breads
- sea salt
- 1 long cucumber, thinly sliced into half moons
- 20 (about 150 g/5½ oz) cherry tomatoes, halved
- 1 red onion, very thinly sliced into half moons
- 2 garlic cloves, finely chopped
- 8 radishes, thinly sliced
- 200 g (7 oz) feto (fermented tofu), crumbled
- olive oil, for drizzling
- freshly squeezed lemon juice, for drizzling
- black pepper
- 30 g (1½ cups) parsley, finely chopped
- 20 g (1 cup) mint leaves
- ground sumac, to serve

Fattoush is a typical Palestinian salad made with fried bread, which you can serve alongside many other dishes. I love to make it when I teach a Middle Eastern cookery workshop. In this recipe, I use deep-fried pita bread but you can also make croutons from stale bread or crackers from left-over sourdough. Anything goes! It's a celebration of fresh and crisp textures that come together in one bite.

METHOD

Heat the sunflower oil in a heavy-based saucepan (it should reach 4 cm/1½ in up the side of the pan) over high heat until it reaches 180°C (350°F). The oil is ready when two wooden chopsticks dipped into the oil sizzle vigorously around their edges.

Cut the pita breads into eight equal triangles — you can also separate them into two single layers, which will result in even crispier bread — then deep-fry for 1–2 minutes, until crisp and golden brown. Drain on paper towel and sprinkle with a generous amount of salt.

Arrange the cucumber, cherry tomato, onion, garlic, radish and feto on a large serving platter. Drizzle generously with olive oil and lemon juice and sprinkle over some salt and a good grind of black pepper. Finish with the parsley, mint, fried bread and a sprinkling of sumac. Ta-dah! ∎

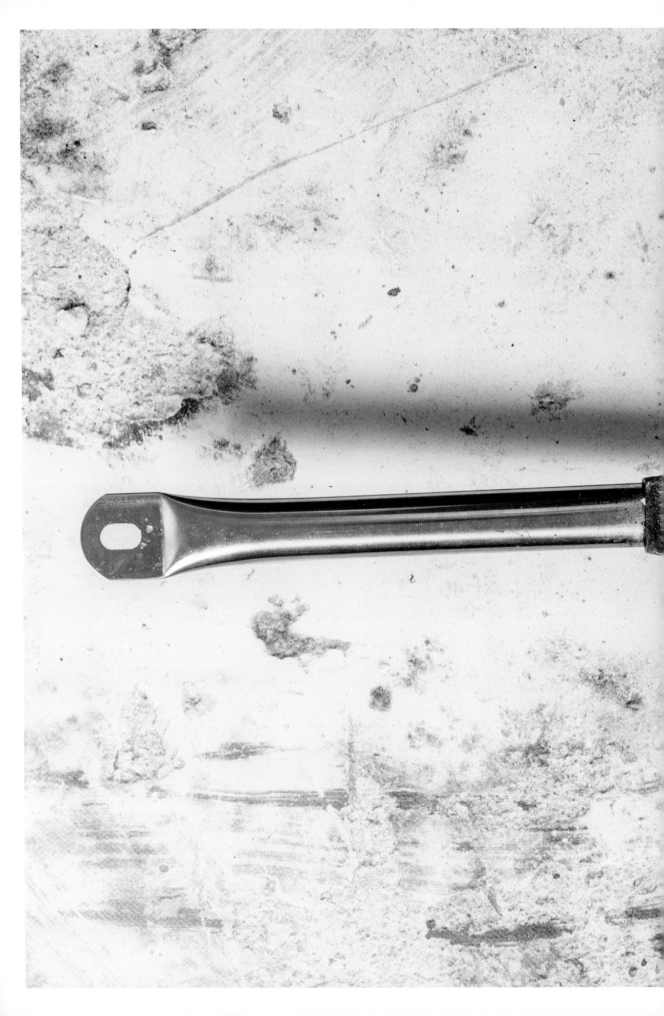

Green salad with grilled nectarines, caramelised cashews & samphire

Serves 4
Preparation time: 20 minutes

INGREDIENTS

- 2 tablespoons mirin
- 2 tablespoons apple juice concentrate
- zest of 1 orange
- 1 drop of shoyu
- 3 nectarines, stones removed, each cut into 8 wedges
- 2 tablespoons olive oil
- 100 g (⅔ cup) raw cashews
- ½ teaspoon smoked paprika
- ½ teaspoon pul biber (Aleppo pepper)
- pinch of sea salt
- 1 tablespoon pure maple syrup
- 120 g (4½ oz) mixed greens, such as rocket (arugula), lettuce and radicchio (or any in-season leaves)
- 70 g (2½ oz) samphire
- edible flowers, to serve (optional)

BALSAMIC DRESSING

- 2 tablespoons balsamic vinegar
- 2 tablespoons umesu
- 2 teaspoons shoyu
- 2 tablespoons pure maple syrup
- 2 tablespoons freshly squeezed lemon juice

When I think about this salad, I think about summer. The days are hot and long and I love to invite people over and load up a huge table with plenty of delicious foods. This salad looks beautiful and tastes wonderful. The nectarines are sweet and comforting and play well with the bitter greens and the salty samphire, and you'll keep on nibbling on the caramelised cashews even after you're full. It is a salad to celebrate life with.

METHOD

Heat a frying pan or chargrill pan over medium–high heat, add the mirin, apple juice concentrate, orange zest and shoyu and bring to a gentle boil. Add the nectarine, increase the heat to high and sauté or grill for 1 minute each side, until the nectarine is just tender, but still al dente. Remove from the heat.

Heat the olive oil in a saucepan over medium heat. Add the cashews and roast for 1–2 minutes, until golden brown. Add the paprika, pul biber, sea salt and maple syrup and sauté for another minute. Immediately remove from the heat and transfer the cashews to a bowl.

For the balsamic dressing, place the balsamic, umesu, shoyu, maple syrup and lemon juice in a bowl and whisk to combine.

Spread the greens over a serving plate and top with the samphire. Delicately arrange the nectarine over the samphire and spoon the dressing over the top. Finish with the cashews and edible flowers (if using) and serve. ∎

SEA
VEGETABLES

SEA

VEGETABLES

Sea vegetables

MINERALS & IRON & CALCIUM

~~~

Seaweed or sea vegetables is a general name for all the edible plants that grow underwater. From my observation, most people still aren't interested in these plants. Of all the foods on earth or in water, seaweed is the richest in minerals. It has enormous amounts of iron and calcium. Each type of seaweed has its own nutritional properties and its own energetic workings.

With the increasing concern about the insufficient amount of iron and calcium in the modern human body and all the physical problems this condition leads to (anaemia, osteoporosis, arthritis, etc.), seaweed may be a simple answer for these concerns. It is definitely a food we should incorporate more into our daily diet. Due to its high mineral content, seaweed forms strong bones, tissues, hair and nails. It provides inner strength but also flexibility due to its fluid and dynamic structure. It is a wonderful food for people who move all the time.

For many people, the taste of seaweed reminds them of sea water and can be new and strange. It is an acquired taste but we can learn to enjoy its flavours over time. Knowledge is required in order to cook seaweed properly and in a delicious way. I hope that these recipes will give you a glimpse into a wonderful culinary world that is much bigger and more extensive than the pages of this cookbook can contain.

Sour tastes, citrus fruits and fruits in general can provide a great contrast to the ocean taste of seaweed and create a pleasurable taste combination. Oil (especially a flavourful oil like extra virgin olive oil or roasted sesame oil) also goes well with seaweed and provides a nice balance to its high mineral content. In this chapter, I mainly use Japanese-style seaweeds, as this is part of my culinary background and field of expertise, but don't hesitate to use these recipes as a base to cook with more local types of seaweed or new varieties that appear on the market. ▪

Wakame salad with tomato, cucumber & salsify

Serves 4
Preparation time: 15 minutes

INGREDIENTS

- sea salt
- 200 g (7 oz) salsify, peeled and halved lengthways, then cut into 5 cm (2 in) pieces
- 2 tablespoons olive oil
- sea salt
- zest of ½ lemon
- ⅛ teaspoon pul biber (Aleppo pepper)
- 25 g (1 oz) instant wakame flakes
- 1 tablespoon roasted sesame oil
- 1 tablespoon shoyu
- 1 tablespoon mirin
- 2 tablespoons freshly squeezed lemon juice
- 50 g (1¾ oz) sunflower seeds
- 300 g (10½ oz) cherry tomatoes, halved
- 1 long cucumber, cut into small chunks
- 1 tablespoon umesu
- 1 tablespoon brown rice vinegar

Enjoy the freshness, earthiness and sea-like taste all in one bite. Salsify's exquisite flavour combines very well with the sea-like flavour of this dish. You get the freshness of the tomato and cucumber, and the sour notes complement them both. Instant wakame is easy to use — you only need to soak it for a few minutes so it's ready in no time. This is a method you can use often to add a seaweed portion to your meal.

METHOD

Bring 1.5 litres (6 cups) of water and a pinch of salt to the boil in a large saucepan. Add the salsify and cook for 10 minutes until soft and al dente, then drain.

Heat 1 tablespoon of the olive oil in a frying pan over high heat. Add the salsify and 1 teaspoon of sea salt and sauté for 1 minute. Add the lemon zest and pul biber and sauté for another minute, until the edges of the salsify are golden. Remove from the heat.

Place the wakame in a small bowl, cover with water and leave to soak for 5–7 minutes, until rehydrated. Drain and squeeze any excess liquid from the wakame, then return it to the bowl and add the sesame oil, shoyu, mirin and 1 tablespoon of the lemon juice and mix well.

Heat the remaining 1 tablespoon of olive oil in a saucepan over medium heat. Add the sunflower seeds and a pinch of salt and roast, stirring constantly, for 2–3 minutes until golden. Immediately remove the sunflower seeds from the pan and set aside.

In a salad bowl, combine the salsify, wakame, sunflower seeds, cherry tomato, cucumber, umesu, remaining 1 tablespoon of lemon juice and the brown rice vinegar. Serve straight away. ∎

Hearty stir-fried greens with cherry tomatoes & wakame

~~~~~~~~~

Serves 4
Preparation time: 20 minutes

INGREDIENTS

- 10 g (¼ oz) instant wakame flakes
- 2 tablespoons roasted sesame oil, plus 1 teaspoon
- 1 tablespoon shoyu, plus 1 teaspoon
- 2 tablespoons mirin, plus 1 teaspoon
- 2 tablespoon plus 1 teaspoon freshly squeezed lemon juice
- 40 g (¼ cup) pine nuts
- 250 g (9 oz) broccoli, cut into small florets
- bunch of turnip greens (about 200 g/7 oz), stalks and leaves roughly chopped
- 1 bok choy (pak choy), cut into large chunks
- 1 garlic clove, finely chopped
- 300 g (10½ oz) cherry tomatoes, halved
- 75 g (2¾ oz) hulled (white) tahini
- ¼ teaspoon sea salt

This is a plentiful dish with greens, tomatoes and seaweed. You can easily replace the turnip greens with kale, chard or spinach or any other seasonal greens.

METHOD

Place the wakame in a small bowl, cover with water and leave to soak for 3–4 minutes, until rehydrated. Drain and squeeze any excess liquid from the wakame, then return it to the bowl and add the 1 teaspoon of sesame oil, the shoyu and mirin, along with 1 teaspoon of the lemon juice. Mix well and set aside.

Place the pine nuts in a saucepan over medium heat and slowly roast, stirring constantly, for 2–3 minutes, until golden brown. Take care not to burn the pine nuts and adjust the heat accordingly. Immediately transfer the pine nuts to a bowl.

Heat the 2 tablespoons of sesame oil in a frying pan over high heat. Add the broccoli and sauté for 1–2 minutes, until the edges of the broccoli are golden brown. Add the turnip greens, bok choy, garlic and tomato, along with a generous grind of black pepper and sauté for 1–2 minutes. Add the 2 tablespoons of mirin and 1 tablespoon of shoyu and sauté for another minute. Remove the pan from the heat, add the wakame mixture and stir it through.

In a small bowl, whisk the tahini, salt and remaining 2 tablespoons of lemon juice. Gradually add 100 ml (3½ fl oz) of water, until the mixture has the consistency of thin yoghurt. If it's too thick, add a little more water; if it's too thin, add a little more tahini.

To serve, scatter the roasted pine nuts over the stir-fried greens and drizzle with the tahini dressing. Enjoy as a side dish with any of the pilafs from the whole grains chapter. ∎

Hiziki-stuffed koya dofu with parsnip & parsley root purée

~~~~~~~~

Serves 4
Preparation time: 45 minutes
Wait time: 30 minutes

INGREDIENTS

- 25 g (1 oz) dried hijiki
- 2 tablespoons roasted sesame oil
- 1 onion, thinly sliced into half moons
- 1 carrot, julienned
- 150 ml (5 fl oz) mirin
- 105 ml (3½ fl oz) shoyu
- 1 tablespoon brown rice vinegar
- black pepper
- 6 pieces (about 100 g/3½ oz) koya dofu (freeze-dried tofu)
- 500–750 ml (2–3 cups) organic sunflower oil, for deep-frying
- 3 tablespoons olive oil
- 2 parsnips (about 400 g/ 14 oz), cut into chunks
- 4 parsley roots (about 400 g/14 oz), cut into chunks
- ½ teaspoon sea salt
- 2 tablespoons freshly squeezed lemon juice
- finely chopped parsley or chives, to serve

I got the idea for this dish from my friend and American macrobiotic teacher, Sheri-Lynn DeMaris, during a macrobiotic conference in the Netherlands. I adapted the recipe slightly to make it richer.

The use of ingredients and the tastes in this dish are quite unusual, so I'd make it when you're looking for something exquisite in terms of different tastes, textures and ingredients. Hiziki is a very strengthening seaweed and very nourishing for your intestines. It is rich, earthy and ocean-like with a good strong bite. This is Japanese traditional cuisine coming together with northern European root vegetables.

At the time of writing, restaurants were closed but when we made this dish we felt as if we were dining at a very exquisite restaurant. To complement your experience, this dish will go very well with some relaxing jazz music in the background.

You can replace the koya dofu with firm tofu, although the dried tofu is tastier.

METHOD

Place the hijiki and 500 ml (2 cups) of water in a pressure cooker, then cover and secure the pressure cooker lid. Place the pressure cooker over high heat and bring to medium pressure. Reduce the heat to low and place the cooker on top of a flame deflector (this will prevent the pressure increasing too much). Cook for 25–30 minutes, then turn off the heat and allow the pressure to release naturally. Alternatively, simmer the hijiki in a saucepan for 45–60 minutes, until very soft. Drain.

Heat the sesame oil in a frying pan over medium–high heat. Add the onion and carrot and sauté for 4–5 minutes. Add the hijiki and sauté for 2 minutes, then add 60 ml (¼ cup) of the mirin, 3 tablespoons of the shoyu, the brown rice vinegar and a generous grind of black pepper. Continue to cook for about 3 minutes, until most of the liquid has evaporated. Remove from the heat and set aside.

Place the koya dofu in a bowl, cover with water and leave to soak for 5 minutes. Squeeze most of the liquid from the koya dofu (there should still be some moisture left), then cut each square diagonally into equal triangles.

Heat the sunflower oil in a heavy-based saucepan (it should reach 4 cm/1½ in up the side of the pan) over high heat until it reaches 180°C (350°F). The oil is ready when two wooden chopsticks dipped into the oil sizzle vigorously around their edges. Deep-fry the koya dofu for 30 seconds on each side, until slightly crisp but not browned. Drain on a plate lined with paper towel.

Using a small knife, make a deep enough incision in each koya dofu triangle to fill with a generous amount of the hijiki mixture.

Heat the olive oil in a saucepan over medium heat. Add the parsnip, parsley root and salt and sauté for about 5 minutes, until the vegetables are caramelised and smell sweet. Add about 400 ml (13½ fl oz) of water and bring to the boil, then reduce the heat to a simmer and cook for 15–20 minutes, until very tender. Remove the pan from the heat and use a stick blender to blend the mixture to a purée.

Meanwhile, fill the koya dofu pockets with the hijiki mixture and set aside. Place 200 ml (7 fl oz) of water in a saucepan, along with the remaining 90 ml (3 fl oz) of mirin, 60 ml (¼ cup) of shoyu and the lemon juice and bring to a gentle simmer. Lay the stuffed koya dofu triangles in the pan and simmer, without boiling, for 2–3 minutes. Gently flip the triangles over and simmer for a further 2–3 minutes to absorb the marinade.

Spread the warm parsnip and parsley root purée on serving plates and top with the stuffed koya dofu and finely chopped parsley or chives. ∎

Wakame, daikon & peach salad

~~~~~~~~~~~

Serves 4
Preparation time: 15 minutes

INGREDIENTS

- 20 g (¾ oz) instant wakame flakes
- 1 tablespoon roasted sesame oil
- 2 teaspoons umesu
- 2 teaspoons brown rice vinegar
- 2 tablespoons mirin
- 2 tablespoons freshly squeezed lemon juice
- ½ daikon, thinly sliced
- 1 large cucumber, deseeded, thinly sliced
- 50 g (1¾ oz) takuan or pickled ginger, julienned
- 2 peaches, stones removed, thinly sliced

This is a light, fresh and simple dish. The fresh and juicy textures of the cucumber, wakame and peach combine perfectly with the wakame.

METHOD

Place the wakame in a small bowl, cover with water and leave to soak for 5 minutes, until rehydrated. Drain and squeeze any excess liquid from the wakame, then return it to the bowl and add the sesame oil, umesu and brown rice vinegar. Mix well and set aside.

Bring the mirin and lemon juice to a gentle boil in a small saucepan. Add the daikon and sauté for 2 minutes, until just tender.

Combine the daikon, cucumber, wakame, takuan or pickled ginger and peach in a salad bowl, and serve. ∎

Seaweed salad with melon & apricots

~~~~~~~~~~

Serves 4
Preparation time: 10 minutes

INGREDIENTS

- 25 g (1 oz) dried mixed seaweed salad
- 1½ tablespoons umesu
- 2 teaspoons roasted sesame oil
- 1½ tablespoons mirin
- 80 ml (⅓ cup) freshly squeezed lemon juice
- 1 tablespoon brown rice vinegar
- 1 long cucumber, peeled in stripes, deseeded, cut into wedges
- 1 melon, seeds removed, cut into wedges
- 4 apricots, stones removed, quartered
- 2 tablespoons apple cider vinegar
- 20 g (⅓ cup) basil leaves
- 20 g (1 cup) mint leaves

This is a great and light way to eat seaweed in the middle of summer. The fruits go very well with the ocean-like flavour of seaweed. Fruit contains vitamin C, which helps the body absorb the minerals in the seaweed. Most people may never have eaten fruits with seaweed in their lives. This makes this salad unusual in its flavours and may require some familiarity with the unique flavours of this plant-based cuisine. I would avoid making it for newcomers.

Note: If summer fruits are not available, you can replace them with other seasonal fruits.

METHOD

Place the dried mixed seaweed salad in a small bowl, cover with water and leave to soak for 5 minutes, until rehydrated. Drain and squeeze any excess liquid from the seaweed, then return to the bowl and add the umesu, sesame oil, mirin, 1½ tablespoons of the lemon juice and brown rice vinegar. Mix well.

In a salad bowl, combine the seaweed mixture, cucumber, melon, apricot, remaining 60 ml (¼ cup) of lemon juice and the apple cider vinegar. Finish with the basil and mint leaves and serve. ∎

PICKLES &

FERMENTATION

Pickles & fermentation

~~~~

In this chapter, I use a variety of techniques to pickle and ferment vegetables. Some of these recipes are for vegetables pickled in liquids that are dominated by acidic vinegar and citrus juice. Other recipes involve fermenting vegetables by putting them in a brine of salt and water and allowing the naturally occurring lactic acid bacteria on the vegetables to produce lactic acid that will preserve the vegetables. The latter technique is often called wild fermentation and is more traditional, older and healthier. It is also more challenging and requires more experience, because the fermentation is spontaneous. You need to acquire a little bit of experience to master this technique. The recipes where I pickle vegetables in vinegar or citrus juice are easier to make and give you more control over the fermentation, but you don't get all the wonderful health benefits that come from wild fermentation.

In wild fermentation (see the recipes on pages 242 and 246), lactic acid bacteria are very active. When we eat the fermented vegetables, we take some of these bacteria into our gut, which helps with digestion and the creation of healthy gut flora. Famous examples of other wild-fermented foods are sauerkraut and kimchi.

Pickled vegetables (see the recipes on pages 234, 237 and 238) don't have the same health benefits, but they are delicious and support digestion as well. Pickles make the meal lighter and add a culinary dimension of sourness. You can serve a small quantity of pickles with every meal. If you have a few types of pickles prepared in your pantry, you can eat a different one every day. ▪

Japanese pickled cucumber

Makes 250 g (9 oz)
Preparation time: 10 minutes
Wait time: 30 minutes and up to overnight

INGREDIENTS

- 1 long cucumber, deseeded, cut into 1 cm (½ in) thick slices
- ½ teaspoon sea salt
- 4 cm (1½ in) piece of ginger, peeled and thinly sliced
- 2 tablespoons shoyu
- 2 tablespoons rice vinegar
- 2 tablespoons pure maple syrup
- 8 cm (3¼ in) long red chilli, thinly sliced
- 2 tablespoons roasted sesame oil

Nothing can satisfy my endless craving for marinated or pickled cucumbers. I made many variations on this recipe for this cookbook and they were all so good that it was hard to choose one to share with you. In the end I chose a recipe that is straightforward and easy to make and has truly irresistible flavours. It's crunchy, it's spicy, it has beautiful Asian flavours, and it makes your mouth water. I bet you won't be able to do anything else if you have a jar of these in your kitchen — other than dream about these cucumbers. Pure pleasure guaranteed.

METHOD

In a bowl, mix the cucumber with the salt and set aside for 30 minutes. Squeeze the water out of the cucumber and discard.

Place the cucumber, ginger, shoyu, rice vinegar, maple syrup, chilli and sesame oil in a zip-lock bag or glass jar, then seal the bag or screw on the lid and leave to marinate for at least 30 minutes and up to overnight.

After marinating, store the cucumbers in the fridge, where they will keep well for up to 1 week. ∎

Israeli-style pickles
in Indian spices

Makes 3 litres (101 fl oz)
Preparation time: 15 minutes
Wait time: 1–3 days

INGREDIENTS

- ½ white cabbage,
  cut into big chunks
- 1 kohlrabi, peeled and
  cut into big chunks
- 1 fennel bulb, cut into big chunks
- ½ daikon, cut into big chunks
- 1 large carrot, cut into big chunks
- 5–6 whole garlic cloves
- 1 long green chilli,
  deseeded, cut into strips
- ½ teaspoon whole
  black peppercorns
- 2½ tablespoons sea salt
- 1 tablespoon ground turmeric
- 1 tablespoon curry powder
- 1 tablespoon ground cumin
- 250 ml (1 cup) apple
  juice concentrate
- 250 ml (1 cup) apple
  cider vinegar
- 125 ml (½ cup) freshly
  squeezed lemon juice

I always find it exciting to make pickles. It's like sending someone on a journey. It's fascinating starting with the vegetables in their raw form and then discovering them later as pickles. In this recipe, the pickling process works very well with the Indian spices. The vegetables here are pickled by submerging them in vinegar and sweet water. The complexity of flavour is really wonderful and reminds me of the pickles they serve at street food stalls in Israel. When I eat them, I am amazed that it is possible to bring sensations, flavours and memories from other continents right into your kitchen. *Beteavon*!

METHOD

Pack the vegetables and garlic into a pickling jar, then add the chilli and peppercorns.

In a large bowl, combine the salt, spices, apple juice concentrate, vinegar, lemon juice and 1 litre (4 cups) of water. Whisk vigorously for 1–2 minutes, until the salt has dissolved, then pour the mixture over the vegetables in the pickling jar. If the jar isn't quite full, top it up with extra water.

Leave at room temperature with the lid very loosely screwed on for 1–3 days. Once the pickles are ready, store them in the fridge or at room temperature. Whichever you choose, they will keep well for 1–2 years. Enjoy their sour flavour and crisp texture! ∎

Pickled red onion

~~~~~~~~

Makes 500 ml (2 cups)
Preparation time: 10 minutes
Wait time: 2 hours and up to overnight

INGREDIENTS

- ½ teaspoon whole black peppercorns
- ½ long red chilli, cut into thin strips
- 5 red onions (about 300 g/10½ oz), cut into very thin half moons
- 60 ml (¼ cup) freshly squeezed lime juice
- 60 ml (¼ cup) freshly squeezed lemon juice
- 60 ml (¼ cup) freshly squeezed orange juice
- 1 tablespoon apple cider vinegar
- ¼ teaspoon sea salt

It's great to have a jar of these fruity pickled onions in the fridge to add a pop of colour and freshness to mealtimes. These Mexican pickles will pump up your meal with a very sour and spicy kick.

METHOD

Place the black peppercorns, chilli and red onion in a pickling jar and add the lime, lemon and orange juice, together with the vinegar and salt. Close the jar and shake well to ensure the onion is covered in the pickling juice — use the handle of a wooden spoon or a chopstick to help push down and submerge the onion, if necessary.

The pickled onion will be ready to eat after 2 hours, or you can leave it overnight. Store in the fridge for up to few months. They rarely spoil. ∎

Pressed salad of beetroot, Chinese cabbage & cucumber

Serves 4
Preparation time: 25 minutes
Wait time: 1 hour and up to 24 hours

INGREDIENTS

- 2 yellow beetroot (beets), peeled and thinly sliced
- 2 target (Chioggia) beetroot (beets), peeled and thinly sliced
- sea salt
- ½ wombok (napa/Chinese cabbage, about 500 g/1 lb 2 oz), cut into big chunks
- 1 long cucumber, peeled in stripes, deseeded and cut into 5 mm (¼ in) strips
- 1 tablespoon roasted sesame oil
- 1 tablespoon pure maple syrup
- 1 tablespoon shoyu
- 1 tablespoon brown rice vinegar
- 1 tablespoon mirin
- 1 tablespoon freshly squeezed lemon juice

In this fermentation technique, I press the vegetables for a few hours or a few days. This speeds up the enzymatic action and the fermentation process. Pressure makes the vegetables more digestible, sweeter and keeps them crisp. You can eat this salad after a few hours or wait for few days. It will stay good for about 5 days outside the fridge. I make it with a delicious Asian dressing full of flavour, which I would love you to try.

METHOD

In a large bowl, combine the beetroot and ½ teaspoon of salt and massage with your hands for about 5 minutes, until the beetroot starts to soften. Transfer the beetroot to a salad press or place a plate on top of the beetroot with a weight on top and leave to one side.

In a large bowl, combine the wombok with ½ teaspoon of salt and massage for 1–2 minutes, until the cabbage starts to soften. Place the wombok on top of the beetroot in a separate layer.

Finally, combine the cucumber with ¼ teaspoon of salt, but don't massage. Place the cucumber on top of the cabbage in a separate layer, then press all the ingredients for at least 30 minutes and up to overnight. Heavily pressed, the salad will become fully submerged in the brine released from the vegetables.

In a small bowl, whisk together the sesame oil, maple syrup, shoyu, brown rice vinegar, mirin and lemon juice.

When you are ready to eat the salad, squeeze as much liquid as possible from the vegetables to help retain their crispness. Discard the water and serve the salad with the dressing. ▪

Spicy pickled red cabbage, red onion, carrot & ginger

~~~~~~~~~~~~

Makes 3 litres (101 fl oz)
Preparation time: 15 minutes
Wait time: 3–7 days

INGREDIENTS

- 1 teaspoon whole
  black peppercorns
- 2 cm (¾ in) piece of ginger,
  peeled and thinly sliced
- 3 bay leaves
- ½ long red chilli,
  cut into thin strips
- ½ red cabbage,
  cut into large chunks
- 8 red onions,
  cut into large wedges
- 3 carrots, cut into long strips
- 10 radishes
- 50 g (1¾ oz) sea salt

This recipe uses wild fermentation, which is the traditional way of making pickles. The vegetables are submerged in a saltwater brine, which allows the lactic acid bacteria (naturally present in all vegetables) to multiply. The lactic acid bacteria creates lactic acid, which preserves the vegetables for a long time. Lactic acid bacteria is wonderful to stimulate and help digestion, add healthy bacteria to our gut flora and eventually make healthy and strong intestines.

METHOD

In a 3 litre (101 fl oz) pickling jar, place the black peppercorns, ginger, bay leaves and red chilli, followed by the red cabbage, red onion, carrot and radishes.

Place the salt in a bowl or jug, add 1 litre (4 cups) of water and whisk for 2–3 minutes, until the salt has completely dissolved. Pour the brine over the vegetables to submerge them — if they're not completely covered in the brine, mix more water and salt, using the same ratio, and pour over the vegetables until they are submerged.

Allow the vegetables to ferment for 3–7 days (see page 249 for more information), then store in the fridge or pantry where they will keep for 1–2 years. ▪

Onion tamari pickles

〜〜〜

Makes 750 ml (3 cups)
Preparation time: 10 minutes
Wait time: 2 days

INGREDIENTS

- 5 medium onions,
  thinly sliced into half moons
- 75 ml (2½ fl oz) tamari soy sauce
- ½ teaspoon black peppercorns
- 2 bay leaves
- 1 tablespoon yuzu juice or
  freshly squeezed lime juice
- 75 ml (2½ fl oz)
  brown rice vinegar

These are crisp, umami and sour pickles for quirky pickle lovers. Give them a try if you crave something salty and savoury. If it wasn't Japanese, I'd say it would fit perfectly in an old-fashioned New York Jewish deli. Taste it and you'll know what I'm talking about.

METHOD

Place the onion, tamari, peppercorns, bay leaves, yuzu and brown rice vinegar in a 1 litre (34 fl oz) pickling jar and use the handle of a wooden spoon or a chopstick to press down and submerge the onion in the pickling liquid. Screw the lid on and set aside to pickle for 2 days, then open and enjoy. The pickled onion will store well in the fridge or pantry for 1–2 years. ∎

A jar of pickles from my sister, Jenia

~~~

Makes 3 litres (101 fl oz)
Preparation time: 10 minutes
Wait time: 3–7 days

INGREDIENTS

- 2 carrots, cut into wedges
- 1 fennel bulb, cut
  into small wedges
- 1 kohlrabi, peeled and
  cut into small wedges
- 6 celery stalks,
  cut into large pieces
- 1 tablespoon black peppercorns
- 2 sprigs of fresh thyme
- 1 teaspoon ground turmeric
- ½ long red chilli, thinly sliced
- 60 ml (¼ cup) freshly
  squeezed lemon juice
- 60 g (2 oz) sea salt

My sister, who gives popular fermentation workshops in Israel (@life_without_medicine), has been bragging about her pickles for years. She says her family devours huge jars of these within a few hours. At last I thought I'd give it a go and try to make them — and they were damn good! The combination of flavours is dynamic, fun and extremely pleasant.

This recipe uses a wild fermentation technique. The process requires more technique and skill than pickling vegetables in vinegar, but the health benefits are enormous and the satisfaction of succeeding is priceless. Besides, what is more prestigious nowadays than being a fermentation geek? Start to ferment and you'll see how many new cool friends you'll make. It is an entire way of life.

METHOD

In a 3 litre (101 fl oz) pickling jar, place the carrot, fennel, kohlrabi, celery, black peppercorns, thyme, turmeric, chilli and lemon juice.

Place the salt in a bowl or jug, add 1.5 litres (6 cups) of water and whisk for 2–3 minutes, until the salt has completely dissolved. Pour the brine over the vegetables to submerge them — if they're not completely covered in the brine, add a little more water until they are submerged.

Allow the vegetables to ferment, with the lid loosely screwed on, for 3–7 days (see page 249 for more information), then store in the fridge or pantry where they will keep for up to 6 months. ▪

About Fermentation

~~~

As a general rule, in the first stages of fermentation, keep the lid only loosely screwed on, so that carbon dioxide can be released. Allow the ingredients to ferment for 3–7 days at room temperature. The duration will depend on the temperature of the room: if the room is very warm, fermentation will only take 2–3 days; in a cold room, you will need to wait for 1 week. Taste the pickles — if you like them, screw the lid on and place the jar in the fridge to slow down the fermentation process. If you would like the pickles to be more sour, leave them longer to ferment at room temperature. You are the one deciding when they are ready!

The first week of fermentation is when most of the carbon dioxide is released (and your kitchen smells like, ahem, you know what …). But after one week you can keep the jar sealed (either inside or outside of the fridge).

TIPS

To avoid mould forming, make sure the ingredients are completely submerged in the liquid. You can do this by placing a weight, a small Tupperware lid or a cabbage stem on top. Sometimes mould does develop, in which case, remove the mould carefully and taste one of the pickles. If it tastes good, don't throw the pickles away! Pickles spoil very rarely, even if mould has developed, because the lactic acid creates a sterile environment, which prevents mould and yeast coming into contact with the ingredients.

Finally, no, you don't need to sterilise your jars and, no, you don't need to boil the brine (the mixture of salt and water). It's just not necessary. The lactic acid bacteria in the vegetables is strong enough to keep pathogens away, as long as they remain submerged in the brine. ∎

FRUITS &

DESSERTS

Fruits & desserts

～～～

Fruits are sweet and fun; they bring joy, light, colour, taste and good energy to a meal. Using fruits in a dessert not only adds more colour, taste and liveliness, it also makes the dessert easier to digest and lighter, because fruits are rich in minerals and vitamins. Instead of ending a meal with a heavy dessert full of sugar and fat and dying from heaviness and melancholy, eating better-quality desserts — like the ones in this chapter — lifts the whole experience of the meal and ends it with a certain elevation, joy and burst of energy.

In this chapter, I try to use local, seasonal fruits for desserts that are homey and not too difficult to make. All the desserts here are vegan and I don't use any refined sugars to sweeten them. In this cookbook, I choose to use better-quality sweeteners that are easier to digest and whose effect is not as harsh on the body as simple refined sugars.

On page 279 you can read more about the main sweeteners that I'm using and the reasons that they're better quality. ▪

Pear crumble with thyme & orange zest

Serves 4
Preparation time: 15 minutes
Wait time: 30 minutes

INGREDIENTS

- 4 pears, peeled, cored and cut into 1–2 cm (½–¾ in) chunks
- 3 tablespoons apple juice concentrate
- drop of shoyu
- zest of 1 orange
- 10 sprigs of thyme

CRUMBLE

- 150 g (1 cup) unbleached plain (all-purpose) flour
- 50 g (1¾ oz) almond flour
- 115 ml (4 fl oz) canola oil or light-tasting olive oil (or other oil for baking, see page 280)
- 115 ml (4 fl oz) pure maple syrup
- ⅛ teaspoon vanilla powder
- pinch of sea salt

Any existential questions about the meaning of life are all answered in the simple and pure moment of eating this modest dessert. 'Why didn't I think of this myself?' you'll ask yourself. 'It's too simple and too good to be true.' You probably could have thought it up, but luckily you bought this book, and luckily you're making it and luckily there is plenty for everyone. After all, pear, thyme and crumble. What on earth can go wrong there? Enjoy every bite and think about me. Promise?

METHOD

Preheat the oven to 170°C (340°F) fan-forced.

If the pears are hard, combine them with the apple juice concentrate and shoyu in a saucepan and bring to a gentle boil over medium heat. Cover with a lid and simmer for 10 minutes until the pear is slightly softened. Transfer to a baking dish and add the orange zest. If the pears are soft, place them directly in a baking dish, add the apple juice concentrate, shoyu, orange zest and thyme and gently toss to combine.

To make the crumble, combine the flour, almond flour, oil, maple syrup, vanilla powder and salt in a bowl and very lightly mix until the ingredients are just combined — don't overmix. The dough will be quite wet. Gently crumble the dough on top of the pear, then transfer to the oven and bake for about 30 minutes, until the crumble is golden and the pear is tender. So simple, so good. ▪

Cherry cake

~~~~~~~~

Serves 12
Preparation time: 10 minutes
Wait time: 35 minutes
Equipment: 30 x 20 cm (12 x 8 in) baking tin

INGREDIENTS

- 265 g (1¾ cups) unbleached plain (all-purpose) flour
- 3 tablespoons crème de tartar (natural baking powder)
- pinch of sea salt
- 265 g (9½ oz) amazake
- 180 ml (6 fl oz) pure maple syrup
- 160 ml (5½ fl oz) canola oil or light-tasting olive oil (or other oil for baking, see page 280), plus extra for greasing
- 500 g (1 lb 2 oz) pitted fresh cherries or 250 g (9 oz) unpitted cherries from a jar

Here's a very good reason to wait for cherry season. My mother used to make this cherry cake the night Yom Kippur finished. Yom Kippur is a Jewish holy day and people fast for the whole 24 hours. I remember the smell of this soft, spongy cherry cake in the house. It's quite light, it's homey and it's so basic that you'll be making and eating it for many years to come. I'm not sure how healthy it was to break a fast with a cake, but it definitely made me want the fast to break quicker and made this moment very pleasurable and memorable.

The nicest fruit to use are fresh cherries in season. Otherwise you can use tinned cherries or any other berries, like blueberries, raspberries or strawberries.

METHOD

Preheat the oven to 175°C (345°F) fan-forced.

In a bowl, whisk together the dry ingredients. In a separate bowl, whisk together the wet ingredients, then whisk the wet mixture into the dry ingredients. You need to do this quickly and smoothly to avoid lumps forming in the batter. Stop mixing as soon as the ingredients are combined to avoid gluten forming, to prevent a heavy cake. Add the cherries and gently mix.

Brush the baking tin with a little oil or line with baking paper to prevent the cake sticking to the tin. Add the cake batter and spread evenly with a spatula, then transfer to the oven and bake for 30–35 minutes, until the top of the cake is golden brown. ∎

Chocolate mousse with cherries

~~~

Serves 8
Preparation time: 30 minutes
Wait time: 1 hour and up to overnight

INGREDIENTS

- 70 g (2½ oz) dark chocolate (100% cacao)
- ¼ teaspoon sea salt
- ¼ teaspoon vanilla powder
- 100 ml (3½ fl oz) soy cream
- 100 ml (3½ fl oz) pure maple syrup
- 60 ml (¼ cup) aquafaba (see below)
- 250 g (9 oz) pitted fresh cherries

This is a classic chocolate mousse made from melted dark chocolate, yet without any dairy or sugar. I use maple syrup to sweeten it and whipped aquafaba to make it airy and light. Aquafaba is a fancy name for the cooking liquid from chickpeas. You can find a method for making aquafaba below, or you can just use the liquid from tinned chickpeas.

AQUAFABA

Makes 300 ml (10½ fl oz)
200 g (7 oz) chickpeas (garbanzo beans)

~~~

Aquafaba is simply the cooking liquid of chickpeas, so you don't necessarily need a special recipe for it. You can just use the liquid from a tin of chickpeas, but for those who want to make it themselves, here is my recipe. You don't need to be too precise, but do make sure your chickpea water is shiny, with an eggy texture that's not too thin. You can use aquafaba in different baking recipes or desserts, such as this chocolate mousse.

Place the chickpeas and 600 ml (20½ fl oz) of water in a pressure cooker and cook for 1 hour 15 minutes under pressure, following the instructions on page 102. Strain the liquid in to a bowl and ta-dah! You have aquafaba. Use the left-over chickpeas for another recipe, such as a salad or hummus, for example. ∎

~~~~~~~~~~~~~~~

METHOD

Bring 3–4 cm (1¼–1½ in) of water to a gentle boil in a saucepan over medium–low heat. Place a heatproof bowl over the pan, making sure the base of the bowl isn't touching the water. This cooking method is called a bain marie, where the steam from the pan heats the ingredients in the bowl. Reduce the heat until the water is only steaming.

Place the chocolate, salt and vanilla in the bowl over the pan and allow the chocolate to melt. Over very low steam (do not let the water boil at all), slowly and carefully whisk in the soy cream and maple syrup. Continue to whisk until the mixture is smooth, then remove the bowl from the pan and allow the chocolate mixture to cool.

Using electric beaters, beat the aquafaba in a bowl for 7–10 minutes, until it resembles meringue. Using a spatula or a wooden spoon, gently fold the meringue into the cooled ganache — this is your mousse.

Divide the mousse among eight bowls and chill in the fridge for at least 1 hour and up to overnight — it will taste even better the next day. The mousse will keep, covered, in the fridge for 5–7 days.

Top the mousse with the cherries and serve. ▪

Pear amazake tart

Serves 12
Preparation time: 25 minutes
Wait time: 30 minutes
Equipment: 25–30 cm (10–12 in) baking tin

INGREDIENTS

- 6 pears, peeled and cored, each cut into 8 wedges
- 60 ml (¼ cup) mirin
- 2 tablespoons apple juice concentrate
- zest of 1 tangerine (or orange)
- drop of shoyu
- 200 g (7 oz) amazake

ALMOND PASTRY

- 240 g (8½ oz) unbleached plain (all-purpose) flour, plus extra for dusting
- 100 g (3½ oz) almond flour
- 1 tablespoon crème de tartar (natural baking powder)
- pinch of sea salt
- 120 ml (4 fl oz) canola oil or light-tasting olive oil (or other oil for baking, see page 280), plus extra for greasing
- 120 ml (4 fl oz) pure maple syrup

This is a very simple and accessible dessert that you can make in no time. You don't need much technique for it. It's a very nice recipe to use as a base for a fruit tart and you can make it with all kinds of fruits. Some pears can be quite hard, depending on the type and season. In this case, you need to pre-cook them. Some pears are over-ripe, and in this case you can use them fresh. You will need to judge the softness or hardness of the pears.

This is the perfect tart to make for your loved ones. The soft pear and the amazake combine well with the flakiness of the dough and give you the tart experience you are looking for. Amazake is a traditional Japanese drink made of fermented rice, but for this recipe I use a thicker, pudding-like version of it.

~~~~~~~~~~

METHOD

Preheat the oven to 170°C (340°F).

If the pears are hard, pre-cook them first: heat the mirin, apple juice concentrate, tangerine zest and shoyu in a saucepan over medium heat. Bring the liquid to a simmer, add the pear, cover and cook for 5–25 minutes (depending on the hardness of the pear), until the fruit is slightly soft but still a little al dente. If the pears are soft, you can skip this step.

To make the almond pastry, place the dry ingredients in a bowl and whisk to combine. In a separate bowl, mix together the oil and maple syrup, then add the wet ingredients to the dry ingredients and whisk quickly. Stop mixing as soon as the ingredients stick together to avoid gluten forming. You can either use the dough immediately or place it in the fridge and chill for 1 hour and up to overnight, which will result in a flakier crust.

Brush the baking tin with a little oil and scatter with flour, or line with baking paper, to prevent the dough sticking. Roll out the dough or use your fingers to push and spread the dough in a thin layer across the base and sides of the tin, about 3 cm (1¼ in) in height, and prick the base with a fork. Don't make the crust too thick, otherwise it won't cook through. If you have some dough left over, use it to make cookies or crumble it on top of the tart before cooking.

Spread a thin layer of amazake over the crust and arrange the pear elegantly on top. If you cooked the pear first, drizzle the cooking liquid over the pear; alternatively, drizzle over 1 tablespoon of the mirin, the apple juice concentrate and shoyu, and scatter with the zest. Transfer to the oven and bake for 30 minutes, until the crust is golden brown. ∎

Apricot, blueberry & amazake galette

〜〜〜〜〜

Serves 12
Preparation time: 20 minutes
Wait time: 1 hour and up to overnight

INGREDIENTS

- 150 g (5½ oz) amazake
- 9 apricots, halved, stones removed
- 2 tablespoons rice syrup
- 90 g (3 oz) fresh blueberries
- 5 sprigs of thyme

GALETTE CRUST

- 280 g (10 oz) unbleached plain (all-purpose) flour
- 100 g (3½ oz) almond flour
- 1 tablespoon crème de tartar (natural baking powder)
- pinch of sea salt
- 120 ml (4 fl oz) canola oil or light-tasting olive oil (or other oil for baking, see page 280)
- 120 ml (4 fl oz) pure maple syrup
- 60 ml (¼ cup) ice-cold water

This recipe is a pleasure for the hands and a joy for the eyes. The crust of this galette is wonderful — sprinkling it with rice syrup makes it very crunchy and caramelised. The blueberries combine beautifully with the apricots. You will need the best apricots in season because they will give the galette tart its dominant character. I like to spread one layer of amazake at the bottom to make it creamier and sweeter, but this is optional, so skip it if amazake is out of your reach. You can also use this recipe as a base for wonderful galette tarts using fruits like peaches, prunes, berries, strawberries, rhubarb or figs.

Note: Use thick amazake with a pudding-like consistency. If only thin, drinking consistency amazake is available, boil it down until it thickens.

METHOD

Preheat the oven to 165°C (330°F) fan-forced.

To make the almond pastry, place the dry ingredients in a bowl and whisk to combine. In a separate bowl, whisk together the oil, maple syrup and ice-cold water, then add the wet ingredients to the dry ingredients and whisk quickly. Stop mixing as soon as the ingredients stick together to avoid gluten forming. Wrap the dough in plastic wrap and chill in the fridge for at least 1 hour and up to overnight.

Line a large baking tray with baking paper. Place the dough on top of the baking paper, then roll it into a 40 cm (16 in) circle. Spread the amazake over the dough, leaving a 5 cm (2 in) border, then top with the apricot, cut-side down. Drizzle with 1 tablespoon of the rice syrup and scatter the blueberries and thyme sprigs evenly over the apricots. Fold the uncovered edge of the dough over the apricot and press the folds together to enclose the filling. Drizzle the remaining 1 tablespoon of rice syrup over the folded crust to help the pastry caramelise, then transfer to the oven and bake for about 40 minutes, until the edges are golden brown and the apricot is soft. ∎

Appelflappen

~~~~~~~~~~~~~

Makes 12
Preparation time: 25 minutes
Wait time: 15 minutes

INGREDIENTS

- 60 ml (¼ cup) pure maple syrup
- drop of shoyu
- 2 apples, cored and diced
- 2 tablespoons raisins
- zest of 1 lemon
- 2 tablespoons kuzu
- 12 x 12 cm (4¾ in) squares of store-bought vegan puff pastry
- 60 ml (¼ cup) rice syrup

These Dutch appleflaps are a delicious sweet pastry perfect for eating on their own or with tea or coffee. You can buy them in most bakeries in the Netherlands but it's also fun to make them at home — especially because you can make them vegan and sugar-free! They are really easy to make when you want something quick and pleasant with no fuss and are best enjoyed just after they come out of the oven, when you can bite into the flaky pastry and discover the crunchy sweet caramel base. The rice syrup that is added during the baking melts and creates a crisp caramel layer on the outside, which goes really well with the sweet tender filling. All in all, it is a very pleasant experience without too much fuss and effort.

Note: You can replace the kuzu with arrowroot or cornstarch.

METHOD

Preheat the oven to 200°C (400°F) fan-forced. Line a baking tray with baking paper.

Heat the maple syrup and shoyu in a saucepan over medium heat. Add the apple, raisins and lemon zest and sauté for 2–3 minutes.

In a small bowl, combine the kuzu and 200 ml (7 fl oz) of water and whisk thoroughly. Add the kuzu mixture to the apple and stir for 1–2 minutes, until the mixture thickens. Remove from the heat.

Spoon 3 tablespoons of the apple mixture in the centre of each pastry square, then fold each square into a triangle, pressing the edges together well to enclose the filling. Transfer the appelflaps to the prepared tray and bake in the oven for 10 minutes.

Remove the tray from the oven and brush each appelflap with about 1 teaspoon of rice syrup, then continue to bake for another 5–10 minutes, until golden brown and crisp. ∎

Dutch doughnuts (Oliebollen)

~~~~~~~~~~~~

Makes 20
Preparation time: 25 minutes

INGREDIENTS

- 450 g (3 cups) unbleached plain (all-purpose) flour
- 400 ml (13½ fl oz) sparkling water
- ¼ teaspoon sea salt
- 2 tablespoons crème de tartar (natural baking powder)
- 1 tablespoon apple cider vinegar
- 150 ml (5 fl oz) rice syrup
- 2 apples, peeled and cored, diced
- zest of 1 orange
- zest of 1 lemon
- 3 tablespoons freshly squeezed lemon juice
- 100 g (3½ oz) raisins
- 500–750 ml (2–3 cups) organic sunflower oil, for deep-frying

The history of Dutch oliebollen dates back 2000 years. No wonder people have kept on eating these for thousands for years — honestly, who doesn't love them? It is easier to make them vegan and without yeast than you might think. I tend to make and eat too many of them before New Year and it takes me another year to digest them and exercise them down. The joy, warmth and pleasure that making these doughnuts brings to the dark and festive winter days is unforgettable.

Sometimes Dutch people make fun of me for making oliebollen. I guess I am not familiar enough with the subtleties of the Dutch culture to understand why. Maybe it's funny, deep-fried, doughy, old-fashioned or whatever else you want to call it, but I'll keep on making oliebollen (full disclosure: also at other times of the year, but don't tell anyone …).

You can alternate or replace the sparkling water with champagne or sparkling wine. If you have a sourdough starter, you can add the starter or the discard to the dough.

~~~~~~~~~~~~~~~~~~~~~

METHOD

In a bowl, combine the flour, sparkling water, salt, crème de tartar, apple cider vinegar and rice syrup. Add the apple, the orange and lemon zest, lemon juice and raisins and mix well. Scoop a big tablespoon of dough out of the bowl, then drop it back in — it should make a 'flop' sound.

Heat the oil in a heavy-based saucepan (it should reach 4 cm/1½ in up the side of the pan) over high heat until it reaches 180°C (350°F). The oil is ready when two wooden chopsticks dipped into the oil sizzle vigorously around their edges.

The easiest way to form the oliebollen is to use an ice-cream scoop. Fill a jar with water and dip the scoop in the water after adding each doughnut to the hot oil. Take a scoop of dough and lower it into the oil, then deep-fry for 5 minutes (you can fry a few doughnuts at a time depending on the size of your pan). Keep an eye on the temperature of the oil — if it's too hot the doughnuts will brown too quickly and the insides will be raw. Allow the doughnuts to sizzle until crisp and golden brown, then repeat with the remaining dough.

Drain the doughnuts on paper towel and be proud that you've made your first oliebollen. ∎

Tahini almond mousse with grilled prunes & caramelised pistachio

Serves 4
Preparation time: 15 minutes

INGREDIENTS

- 70 g (2½ oz) white almond butter
- 120 g (4½ oz) Medjool dates, pitted
- 300 g (10½ oz) silken tofu
- 1 teaspoon freshly squeezed lemon juice
- 40 ml (1¼ fl oz) almond milk
- 80 g (2¾ oz) hulled (white) tahini
- sea salt
- 60 ml (¼ cup) apple juice concentrate
- 4 prunes, halved, stones removed
- zest of 1 orange
- 40 g (1½ oz) shelled pistachios, roughly chopped
- 2 tablespoons pure maple syrup

This is a wonderful dessert with a nice Middle Eastern vibe. The tahini, almond butter and silken tofu create a very creamy and indulgent mousse, and the caramelised pistachios taste so good. You can grill any fruits that are in season. I used prunes but you can also use apricots. This combination is joyful, colourful and something you can serve to guests with great pride. It's also quite an easy dessert to make and it definitely doesn't require a lot of technique.

Tip: Freeze the mousse mixture a few hours before it's needed and blend just before serving. The mousse will turn into delicious ice-cream. This is way better than serving it at room temperature!

METHOD

To make the almond mousse, place the almond butter, dates, silken tofu, lemon juice, almond milk, tahini and a pinch of salt in a food processor and process until combined.

Heat the apple juice concentrate in a chargrill pan over medium–high heat. Add the prunes, cut side down, then sprinkle with the orange zest and a pinch of salt and grill for 2–3 minutes on each side.

Heat the pistachios in a saucepan over medium heat and roast, stirring constantly, for 2–3 minutes, until golden brown. Add the maple syrup and a pinch of salt and stir until most of the maple syrup has evaporated.

Spoon the almond mousse onto small serving plates in neat mounds, then top with two prune halves and sprinkle over the caramelised pistachios. ∎

Let's get a little technical ...

~~~~

Maple syrup

Maple syrup is made from the sap that comes out of maple trees from the end of the winter until the beginning of spring, and is then boiled down. Because it's naturally sourced from maple trees and not refined, it still has quite a high mineral (manganese) and B group vitamin content, which helps with the digestion of simple sugars.

~~~~

Rice syrup

Rice syrup is made by mixing digestive enzymes with cooked sweet rice. Traditionally, rice syrup is made by mixing sprouted barley with cooked rice. The sprouts break down the complex sugars in the rice to produce simple sugars, which results in a honey-like syrup. Because it's made from brown rice, it contains vitamins and minerals that support digestion, and its effect on the body is not as extreme as that of processed sugar.

~~~~

Apple juice concentrate

Apple juice concentrate is made from boiled-down apple juice, so it still contains all the minerals and vitamins from the fruits.

Oil

In the Netherlands, I often use organic deep-frying oil for baking. It might sound strange but this sunflower oil, which has been filtered to produce a thin, neutral-tasting and smelling oil, is very suitable for baking. It is also good value for money. Other oils that you can use for baking include safflower oil, canola oil, rapeseed oil, grapeseed oil, mild-tasting olive oil, almond oil, rice germ oil, rice oil, rice bran oil, corn oil and corn germ oil. I avoid using coconut oil because it contains saturated fat (similar to animal fat) and has a blocking and weakening effect on the body. ∎

Rice pudding with almond crunch & mango cream

~~~~~~~~~~

Serves 4
Preparation time: 30 minutes

INGREDIENTS

- 150 g (5½ oz) arborio rice, koshihikari (sushi) rice or white round rice
- pinch of sea salt
- 4 tablespoons almond paste
- 90 ml (3 fl oz) soy cream
- 12 cardamom pods, bashed open and seeds removed
- 200 ml (7 fl oz) rice syrup
- zest of 1 lemon
- 1 tablespoon freshly squeezed lemon juice
- ½ teaspoon vanilla powder

ALMOND CRUNCH

- 40 g (1½ oz) flaked almonds
- 20 g (¾ oz) almond flour
- 20 g (¾ oz) unbleached plain (all-purpose) flour
- 50 ml (1¾ fl oz) pure maple syrup
- 2 tablespoons olive oil
- big pinch of sea salt
- ½ teaspoon ground cinnamon

MANGO CREAM

- 1 mango, peeled and cut into chunks
- 2 tablespoons freshly squeezed lime juice

You can make this dessert with apricots instead of mangoes if they are local and in season, but I couldn't resist mango because it tastes so good. The contrast of all the textures and temperatures go well together. The rice pudding is creamy, soft, comforting, very homey and a little bit old-fashioned. The almond crunch is crisp and the mango cream is fresh, sour and uplifting. This is quite a simple recipe to make, but it is a festive and enjoyable dessert and I'm sure everyone who tastes it will love it.

METHOD

Preheat the oven to 170°C (340°F) fan-forced.

Place the rice in a saucepan, cover with water and wash lightly, then drain and repeat, if necessary, until the water runs clear. Place the rice back in the pan and add 500 ml (2 cups) of water and the salt, then bring to the boil over medium–high heat. Reduce the heat to a simmer and cook the rice for 18 minutes. Add the almond paste, soy cream, cardamom seeds, rice syrup, lemon zest and juice and vanilla powder and stir well. Simmer, stirring, for a further 15 minutes, until the mixture has a rice pudding–like consistency.

For the almond crunch, place the flaked almonds, almond flour, plain flour, maple syrup, olive oil, salt and cinnamon in a bowl and mix well. Line a baking tray with baking paper and spread the almond mixture on top in an even layer. Transfer to the oven and bake for 10–15 minutes, until dark brown.

To make the mango cream, place the mango and lime juice in a bowl and use a stick blender to blend until smooth. Alternatively, you can do this in a blender or a food processor.

Divide the rice pudding among four glasses (martini glasses or jars work well), then add a layer of almond crunch, which you can break over the top of the rice pudding. Finish with a layer of the mango cream. You're ready to go! ∎

Sample menus

~~~

Here are some examples of simple daily menus that you can prepare in 30–45 minutes, which will provide you with a healthy and nourishing plant-based meal.

1 ~~~
— Brown rice pilaf with broccoli & shiitake mushrooms   P 34
— Wakame salad with tomato, cucumber & salsify   P 217

2 ~~~
— A big wok of soba noodles   P 71
— Pressed salad of beetroot, Chinese cabbage & cucumber   P 240

3 ~~~
— Barley pilaf with cherry tomatoes & seitan   P 42
— Pear, basil & roasted almond salad   P 192

4 ~~~
— Black bean stew with pumpkin & fried seitan   P 84
— A salad of red cabbage, apple & toasted chilli peanuts   P 157

5 ~~~
— A light miso soup with plenty of greens   P 195
— Japanese pickled cucumber   P 234
— Basics: pressure cooker brown rice   P 69

6 ~~~
— Soba noodles with carrot & ginger tempura in clear Japanese broth   P 67
— Brown rice pilaf with cherry tomatoes & chanterelles   P 37

7 ~~~
— Chilli sin carne with kidney beans, guacamole & fried tortilla chips   P 91
— Pickled red onion   P 238

8 〜〜〜
— Seitan wraps with oyster mushrooms & sundried tomato pesto   P 98

〜〜〜

Here are two examples of impressive festive menus that you can
prepare for guests and your family.

1 〜〜〜
— An abundance of greens with roasted hazelnuts & tomato tahini   P 201
— Farro salad with pumpkin, colourful beetroot & cherry tomatoes   P 31
— Jerusalem salad   P 96
— Caramelised sweet potatoes with thyme   P 176
— Tahini almond mousse with grilled prunes & caramelised pistachio   P 276

2 〜〜〜
— Fattoush   P 206
— Lentil stew with roasted oyster mushrooms, samphire &   P 108
  panko-fried seitan
— Roasted fennel with pumpkin seed tahini   P 150
— Chocolate mousse with cherries   P 260

Special ingredients

~~~~~

You may have noticed that I use a lot of special Japanese ingredients. My style is heavily influenced by the Japanese style of cooking and I think these ingredients taste amazing. They're also very good for our health and digestion. They will also bring variation and depth of flavour into your cooking. I recommend buying good organic quality, as that will make a world of a difference to the quality of your cooking.

Unfortunately, you can't yet find these ingredients in every supermarket but, luckily, they're becoming more popular and are available in many organic stores. There is also a list of online stores on page 291 where you can find most of these ingredients.

Amazake
~~~~~
Fermented sweet rice pudding. If this is not available, you can leave it out of the tarts on pages 264 and 268 and use banana mash or apple puree for the cherry cake on page 257. See 'Shops & online stores' on page 291. Amazake comes in both a thin, drinking consistency and a thicker, pudding-like a consistency. In this cookbook, I use the thicker amazake. If only the thin amazake is available, boil it down until it thickens.

### Brown short-grain rice
~~~~~
You can find this in most organic stores. If it is not available, use any other type of brown rice.

Brown sweet rice
~~~~~
A sticky version of brown rice. If it is not available, you can replace it with normal brown round rice. See 'Shops & online stores' on page 291.

### Crème de tartar
~~~~~
Powder made from the residues of wine fermentation. This is a good alternative to baking powder. You will find it in most organic food stores. If it is not available, you can substitute normal baking powder in a smaller amount (about 65% of the amount in the recipe). It is also sold as cream of tartar.

Daikon
〜〜〜
A root vegetable with sharp taste, often called white radish or Japanese radish. You can find this in organic markets or Asian stores. If it is not available, replace it with radish, kohlrabi or turnip.

Dashi
〜〜〜
Japanese broth powder. This is usually made from fish flakes, but if you're lucky you can find delicious vegan dashi made from kombu and shiitake mushrooms. If it is not available, replace it with normal bouillon powder or salt or blend kombu and shiitake to a thin powder in a food processor yourself. See 'Shops & online stores' on page 291.

Ginger pickles
〜〜〜
Japanese pickled ginger. This is available in most organic food stores. Look for a variety that does not contain sugar. See 'Shops & online stores' on page 291.

Hijiki
〜〜〜
A type of hard seaweed. You can find this in organic food stores and Asian stores.

Kombu
〜〜〜
A type of hard seaweed with a strong umami flavour. You can find this in most organic stores and Asian stores.

Koya dofu
〜〜〜
Freeze-dried tofu. This has a more satisfying texture then normal tofu. Soak it in water and squeeze before use. If it is not available, you can replace it with normal tofu or smoked tofu. See 'Shops & online stores' on page 291.

Kuzu
〜〜〜
A starch from the kuzu root. This makes dishes thicker and very medicinal for the intestines. You can find it at most organic food stores.

Mirin
〜〜〜
Japanese rice wine for cooking. This gives a sweet flavour to dishes. You can find it in all organic stores.

Miso
〜〜〜
Japanese paste of fermented beans. This adds a salty and umami flavour to dishes. You can purchase it in all organic food stores. There are few types of miso:

Genmai miso (dark miso)
〜〜〜
Long-fermented miso with brown rice; salty and strong umami

Mugi miso (dark miso)
〜〜〜
Long-fermented miso with barley; salty, umami and a bit sour

Shiro miso (white miso)
〜〜〜
Quickly fermented miso with white rice; light and sweet.

Mixed seaweed salad
〜〜〜

A dry mixture of few kinds of seaweeds. You can find this in some organic stores, or at some of the stores listed on page 292.

Nanami (shichimi) togarashi
〜〜〜

Japanese chilli mixture of seven spices. This gives a spicy taste to dishes. You can find it in most Asian stores. If it is not available, you can replace it with chilli powder, pul biber (Aleppo pepper) or piri-piri.

Pul biber (Aleppo pepper)
〜〜〜

Syrian chilli pepper. This has a sweet and sour flavour. You can find it in Middle Eastern stores. If it is not available, you can replace it with normal chilli flakes or powder (but use less, because pul biber is relatively mild).

Seitan
〜〜〜

Wheat protein. This is available in most organic stores. Look for varieties with soft and fluffy textures. Some are as hard as a shoe (and that's not a compliment).

Shoyu
〜〜〜

Natural, traditionally fermented soy sauce. This gives a salty and umami flavour to dishes. You can get it in all organic stores. If it is not available, you can replace it with normal commercial soy sauce.

Sumac
〜〜〜

Sour-tasting Middle Eastern spice with a purple colour. You can find this in most Middle Eastern shops. If it is not available, just leave it out.

Takuan
〜〜〜

Japanese long-fermented daikon. You can find this in some Asian stores. If it is not available, skip it or replace with ginger pickles. See 'Shops & online stores' on page 291.

Umesu
〜〜〜

Often called plum vinegar or umeboshi vinegar. This is not a vinegar, but rather the liquid that remains after the fermentation of umeboshi (Japanese sour salted plums). It has a light sour and salty flavour. If it is not available, replace it with salt and vinegar, or salt and lemon juice. You can also use a mashed umeboshi plum or umeboshi paste instead. See 'Shops & online stores' on page 291.

Shops & online stores

WHERE TO BUY
SPECIALIST INGREDIENTS

~~~

There are many online stores where you can find the more specialised ingredients used in this book. However, don't be shy about being creative and replacing a weird ingredient I use with something you think will fit. The recipes in the book are pretty flexible — you shouldn't be scared to make them your own. In some places, I gave suggestions about variations for harder-to-find ingredients. Feel free to use these.

In general, all the Japanese ingredients I use are organic quality and you can find most of them in organic food stores. You can also go to supermarkets, but the quality of the ingredients sometimes won't be as good.

For Middle Eastern spices and special ingredients, I usually go to Middle Eastern shops.

For fruits and vegetables, try to buy the best organic quality you can, ideally from a farmers' market, directly from the farmer or grow it yourself (more easily said than done) — but produce from an organic shop is also fine. I would avoid doing regular shopping in the normal supermarket, because the quality of the products is often lower and chemicals and pesticides are often used on the fruit and vegetables. For optimum health and vitality, strive to buy the best quality ingredients.

On the following page are some online stores that have some of the more specialised Japanese macrobiotic ingredients like umesu, amazake, koya dofu, unpasteurised miso and shoyu, hiziki, kuzu, mirin, kombu, dashi, sweet brown rice and takuan. You can also order most of these products online by searching the title of the ingredient using a search engine.

Australia & New Zealand
~~~

— buyorganicsonline.com.au
— ceres.co.nz
— chantalorganics.co.nz
— enmore.tasteorganic.com.au
— enokidomiso.com.au
  (organic miso and shoyu)
— happyandhealthy.co.nz
— huckleberry.co.nz
— naturallyorganic.co.nz
— onlinestore.wholefoodshouse.com.au
— riceculture.com.au
  (organic miso)
— santosorganics.com.au

Europe
~~~

— arche-naturkueche.de
— e-sunfood.cz
— provida.pt
— tampopofoods.com
  (delivers worldwide)
— violey.com

Hong Kong, China
~~~

— macrofoods.com.hk
— shop.weherbhk.com

Israel
~~~

— amberpremium.com

North America
~~~

— avenue.ambrosia.ca
— naturalimport.com
— shop.goldminenaturalfoods.com
— southrivermiso.americommerce.com
  (organic miso)
— store.edenfoods.com

United Kingdom
~~~

— buywholefoodsonline.co.uk
— clearspring.co.uk
— planetorganic.com
— realfoods.co.uk
— therealfoodcompany.org.uk

Sources &
further reading

FIND OUT MORE ABOUT A HEALTHY
LIFESTYLE & MACROBIOTICS

~~~~

The nutritional information and approach in this book is
based on a few resources and disciplines, including the:

— Harvard School of Medicine food chart
— Mediterranean diet
— Macrobiotic diet

The information about the connection between a plant-based
wholefood diet and the prevention and reversal of chronic sickness
is based on the following sources:

Physicians Committee for Responsible Medicine
~~~~

This American organisation of 12,000 doctors, under the direction
of Dr Neal Barnard, supports a plant-based diet as the main tool
to prevent and reverse chronic sickness. Visit the website (pcrm.org)
for the latest research on the prevention of diabetes, cancer, obesity,
heart disease and more.

How not to die — by Dr Michael Greger (2015)
~~~~

This is an extensive book with ample research on how a plant-based
wholefood diet can prevent all common Western sickness.

The China study — by T. Colin Campbell & Thomas M. Campbell (2005)
~~~~

This 20-year study looked at mortality rates from cancer and other
chronic diseases in China. The authors conclude that people who eat
a predominantly vegan wholefood diet — avoiding animal products
as a source of nutrition and reducing their intake of processed foods
and refined carbohydrates — will escape, reduce or reverse the
development of numerous diseases.

I often refer to and talk about the energies of food and their effect on our body and mental state. These principles are based on the macrobiotic way of eating and thinking. These resources describe the macrobiotic philosophy:

The macrobiotic way — by Michio Kushi (2004)

A beginner's book that explains the fundamentals of the macrobiotic diet and lifestyle.

The book of macrobiotics: the universal way of health, happiness, and peace — by Michio Kushi (2012)

An in-depth extensive book that explains the Eastern philosophy of macrobiotics.

Mayumi's kitchen — by Mayumi Nishimura (2012)

A 12-day menu plan with simple macrobiotic recipes from the Japanese macrobiotic chef who cooked for Madonna.

Thanks

~~~~

I would like to thank this very small but oh so great group of people who made this book possible.

Anthea Bull, Mulan Koopmans and Daphne van Schaijk, the wonderful interns who joined me in this adventure and helped me to write all these recipes. As I was cooking, I was explaining what I was doing and they were writing, tasting and commenting. When I say 'we' in the recipe intros, it is because, thanks to them, I was never alone while writing this book.

Hendrik de Leeuw and Emile Blomme from Bertram and de Leeuw publishers, Netherlands, who gave me the wonderful opportunity to write this book, believed in me and encouraged me to bring the best out of myself. It is a great pleasure working with you!

The super-professional team from Smith Street Books, Australia, Paul McNally, Aisling Coughlan, Lorna Hendry, Lucy Heaver and Ariana Klepac, who gave me the unique opportunity to publish these recipes in English and share them with the world. What an honour to finally work with you. You were on my list for a long time.

Lester Hekking, the top literary agent from Sebes & Bisseling Literary Agency, who worked very hard and supported me in the process of writing this book.

Yannick van Leeuwaarde for your exceptional photography, great talent and amazing taste. Thank you for making this book so much more beautiful with your photography. What an honour to work with an upcoming talent like you!

Maartje Pasman, my dear, dear, kind and positive angel, who translated these recipes from English to Dutch for the Dutch publication of the book. Thank you so much. Your generosity, love and dedication makes me cry as I write these lines. Thank you, thank you, thank you.

Isabel van der Weijden with your sharp instincts, insight and feedback. Thank you so much for advising me through the whole process and making things so much clearer and right. Thank you for your good will!

Kim Waterlander and Marjanne Kuipers from Stukk Design for your incredible talent, bursts of creativity and patience and hard work in making this beautiful design.

Ingrid Berger Myhre, thank you for being there, always ready, always listening, always supporting. There were times I was about to collapse and give up, but our sincere talks and your wisdom and encouragement have carried me through these challenging times.

To all my incredible clients, to all my readers, to my friends and followers who tested recipes. Thank you for supporting my work for the last 10 years and especially during the extremely difficult pandemic times. Because of your support and because you asked me to cook for you and bought my books, I have survived this period. I can't tell you how much your support means to me. Without you, my work is not possible. We are doing this together. Let's make the world a better place. ▪

My little plant-based kitchen

EPILOGUE

〰

My kitchen is where I create, where I aspire, where I am happy and sad, where I love and I miss, where I plan and I discuss. It's where small and big dreams come true, dreams of hot dishes, of far places, of people not yet met. My kitchen is the biggest kitchen in the world. Here is where I lose myself in fantasies, tell stories, turn the music up too loud, sing songs as if no one can hear, dance as if no can see, fall in love, miss my family, meet my friends, work hard and eventually here is where I take a break and after hours, days and weeks of cooking, here is where I almost fall asleep.

In this tiny kitchen, I have hosted friends and guests from all over the world. Here is where flamboyant adventures were told with stirring passion, here is where never-before-told secrets were revealed, here is where I finally sat quietly after serving everyone, looking my guests straight in the eyes. Here there are dreams to be dreamt, stories to be told, songs to be sung.

In my plant-based kitchen, pans are steaming, candles are burning, music is playing, guests are laughing, fruits are ripening and cucumbers are fermenting. I come here when I am happy and when I am sad. Here I celebrate my victories and here I seek comfort for my failures. When the outside world feels hostile and unaccommodating, my little plant-based kitchen is always there for me. In this tiny city kitchen I dare to dream big, to make grand plans and travel far to undiscovered places, ingredients and smells. Every little box and bag conveys stories of countries, encounters, love affairs, farewells, successes and failures. In my little plant-based kitchen, I make plans, I dream dreams, I make wishes. I make little notes: 'Make the world a better place to be'. ▪

Index

almond flour 254, 264, 268, 282
almond paste 48, 180, 276, 282
almonds 31, 50, 101, 182, 192, 282
amazake 257, 264, 268
apple 157, 182, 198, 270, 273
apricot 228, 268, 276
apricot, dried 48, 52
aquafaba 260
arugula *see* rocket
asparagus 201
aubergine *see* eggplant
avocado 91, 124

barley/pearl barley 41
basil 101, 159, 192, 228
bean sprouts 110
beans 93, 103; *see also*
kidney beans; broad beans;
white beans; black beans
beetroot 31, 138, 185, 240
bell pepper *see* capsicum
berries *see* blueberries; cranberries
black beans 84
blueberries 268
bok choy 218
bread 96, 126, 206;
see also tortilla wraps
broad beans 81
broccoli/broccolini 34, 71,
169, 195, 201, 205, 218

cabbage 157, 185, 195,
198, 205, 237, 240, 242
capers 138
capsicum 91, 165
cashews 45, 138, 210
cauliflower 41, 126, 169
celeriac 135
celery 246
cherries 260, 257
chickpeas 96, 260
chillies 91, 124, 129, 159, 234
cilantro *see* coriander
chocolate 260
cinnamon 50
coriander 110, 129, 159
courgette *see* zucchini
couscous 41
cranberries 157
cucumber 45, 96, 110, 124,
135, 206, 217, 228, 234, 240

daikon 131, 226, 237
dashi powder 67, 131, 151, 195
dates 276
dumplings 54, 55

eggplant 170
edible flowers 210

farro 31
fava beans *see* broad beans
feto *see* tofu, fermented

garbanzo beans *see* chickpeas
ginger 52, 54, 67, 71, 110,
131, 135, 195, 205, 234, 242
ginger pickles 45, 226, 289
guacamole 91, 92, 124

harissa 81, 83
hazelnuts 201
hijiki 223

Jerusalem artichoke 138, 180

kidney beans 91
kohlrabi 98, 152, 180, 182, 237, 246
kombu 67, 93, 131, 152
koya dofu *see* tofu, dried

leek 37, 126
lemon 142
lemon, preserved 81
lentils 108
lettuce 86, 210
lime 142

mango 282
maple syrup 31, 45, 48, 71, 91, 110,
157, 192, 210, 234, 240, 254, 257, 260,
264, 268, 270, 276, 279, 282
melon 228
millet 185
mint 206, 228
miso 131, 135, 138, 142, 195
mushrooms 37, 38, 54, 64,
98, 108, 114, 165, 169, 205
mushrooms, dried 34, 67, 152

~~~

nectarine 210
noodles 45, 67, 71; *see also* pasta
nori 45, 117
nuts *see* almonds;
cashews; hazelnuts

~~~

oatmeal 48
olives 41, 129
onion 165, 244
onion, red 86, 96, 206, 238, 242
onion, spring 195, 205
orange 45, 166, 254

~~~

parsley 41, 96, 129, 159, 206
parsley root 223
parsnips 126, 129, 145, 223
pasta 64, 101; *see also* noodles
peach 226
peanut butter 110
peanuts 157
pear 192, 254, 264
peas, green 185; *see also* snow peas
pesto 98, 101
pickles 86, 98
pine nuts 34, 41, 218
pistachios 276
plums 268
polenta 38
potato 117, 165
puff pastry 270
pumpkin 31, 84, 101, 152
pumpkin seeds 150

~~~

radish 45, 98, 185, 242
raisins 50, 270, 273
rice 34, 37, 50, 52, 69, 282
rocket 41, 129
rutabaga *see* swede

~~~

salsify 124, 142, 217
scallion *see* onion, spring
seitan 41, 54, 84, 98, 108, 114, 165
silverbeet 201
soba noodles 45, 67, 71
spinach 38, 54
swede 159
sweetcorn 41, 96
Swiss chard *see* silverbeet

~~~

tahini 86, 96, 131, 150,
170, 174, 185, 201, 218, 276
tamari 244
tempeh 86, 91
thyme 176, 154
tofu 110
tofu, dried (koya dofu) 78, 117, 152, 223
tofu, fermented (feto) 96, 129, 206
tofu, silken 135, 138, 145, 276
tomato 31, 37, 41, 135, 165, 91, 96,
108, 142, 159, 185, 201, 206, 217, 218
tortillas 86, 91, 98
turnip 98
turnip greens 129, 218

~~~

white beans 78, 101

~~~

zucchini 41, 174

Smith Street Books

~~~

Original title *Plantaardig, 80 voedzame en smakelijke recepten uit de keuken van een gepassioneerde chef-kok*
First published in 2021 by Bertram + de Leeuw Uitgevers, The Netherlands www.bertramendeleeuw.nl

This edition published in 2023 by Smith Street Books (Naarm) Melbourne | Australia | smithstreetbooks.com

ISBN: 978-1-9227-5413-4

TEXT AND RECIPES
Alexander Gershberg

PHOTOGRAPHY
Yannick van Leeuwaarde

FOOD STYLING
Alexander Gershberg

For Smith Street Books

EDITORS
Lucy Heaver, Tusk Studio and Lorna Hendry

GRAPHIC DESIGN
Stukk Design

EXTERNAL ADVISER
Isabel van der Weijden

ORIGINAL ENGLISH TRANSLATION
Alexander Gershberg

PROOFREADER
Ariana Klepac

Printed & bound in China by C&C Offset Printing Co., Ltd.

Book 248
10 9 8 7 6 5 4 3 2 1